INTRODUCING

Shakespeare

Nick Groom and Piero

Edited by Richard Appignanesi

ICON BOOKS UK   TOTEM BOOKS USA

Published in the UK in 2001
by Icon Books Ltd., Grange Road,
Duxford, Cambridge CB2 4QF
E-mail: info@iconbooks.co.uk
www.iconbooks.co.uk

Published in the USA in 2001
by Totem Books
Inquiries to: Icon Books Ltd.,
Grange Road, Duxford,
Cambridge CB2 4QF, UK

Sold in the UK, Europe, South Africa
and Asia by Faber and Faber Ltd.,
3 Queen Square, London WC1N 3AU
or their agents

Distributed to the trade in the USA by
National Book Network Inc.,
4720 Boston Way, Lanham,
Maryland 20706

Distributed in the UK, Europe,
South Africa and Asia by
Macmillan Distribution Ltd.,
Houndmills, Basingstoke RG21 6XS

Distributed in Canada by
Penguin Books Canada,
10 Alcorn Avenue, Suite 300,
Toronto, Ontario M4V 3B2

Published in Australia in 2001
by Allen & Unwin Pty. Ltd.,
PO Box 8500, 83 Alexander Street,
Crows Nest, NSW 2065

ISBN 1 84046 262 0

Originating editor: Richard Appignanesi

Printed and bound in the UK
by Biddles Ltd., Guildford and King's Lynn

dentifying Shakespeare

Shakespeare is performed, read and studied in most parts of the world today. Why is there such interest – or, more important – why *should* there be any interest in an English writer from Stratford who died nearly 400 years ago? Is it because he is often said to be the world's "greatest" writer? In other words, he has transcended the limits of time and place to become a figure of global significance. That is an astonishing claim. We can begin to understand this phenomenon by asking first: "Who is the *real* William Shakespeare?"

Born on St George's Day

23 April 1564, St George's Day: William Shakespeare is born in Stratford-upon-Avon. The National Poet arrives on the day celebrating the canonization of the patron saint of England – or did he? Historical facts have been massaged to support national or cultural interests. The only reliable evidence is that Shakespeare was baptized on 26 April 1564, so he could have been born on the 21st, or the 22nd, or the 23rd – it was later "Bardolaters" (worshippers of "The Bard") who agreed that Shakespeare's birthday was St George's Day, marrying the nation to his verse.

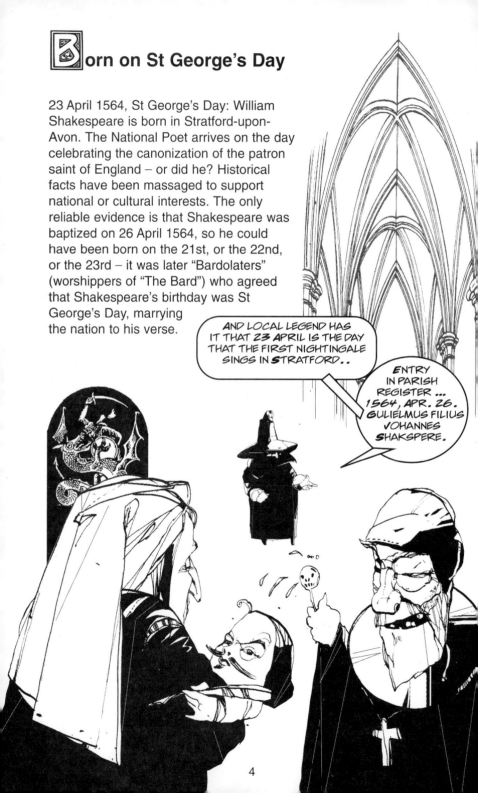

AND LOCAL LEGEND HAS IT THAT 23 APRIL IS THE DAY THAT THE FIRST NIGHTINGALE SINGS IN STRATFORD..

ENTRY IN PARISH REGISTER ... 1564, APR. 26. GULIELMUS FILIUS JOHANNES SHAKSPERE.

He was the eldest son of John Shakespeare, a glovemaker, who had married the Catholic girl Mary Arden in about 1557.

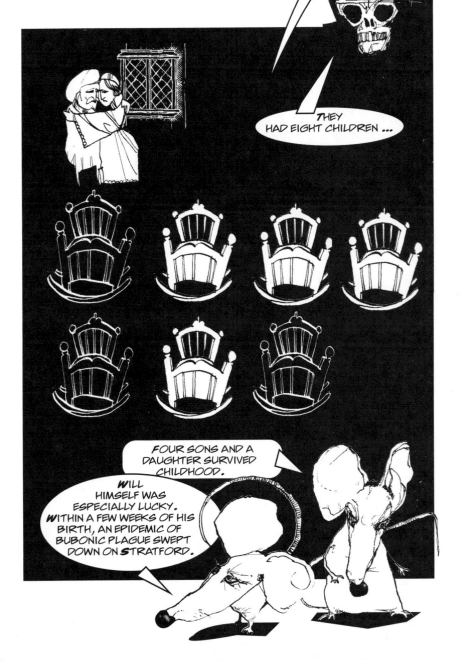

THEY HAD EIGHT CHILDREN ...

FOUR SONS AND A DAUGHTER SURVIVED CHILDHOOD.

WILL HIMSELF WAS ESPECIALLY LUCKY. WITHIN A FEW WEEKS OF HIS BIRTH, AN EPIDEMIC OF BUBONIC PLAGUE SWEPT DOWN ON STRATFORD.

amily Ambitions

Will's father, the glover of Henley Street, may not have been an educated man. He could probably read, but couldn't write much more than his accounts (though his wife signed documents with an elaborate mark that demonstrates she had some facility with a quill pen).

But in 1570, as Will was about to start at school, his respectable father was fined for breaking money-lending laws, and the family fortunes began to decline. Two years later, he was accused of "wool brogging": illegally dealing in fleeces. His eldest son was certainly privy to these goings-on – he remembered the details for the rest of his life.

Let me see. Every 'leven wether tods, every tod yields pound and odd shilling; fifteen hundred shorn, what comes the wool to?

This reference occurs in Shakespeare's play
The Winter's Tale, Act IV, scene iii, lines 32-4.
In modern English:
Every eleven rams yield a tod of 28lbs, worth 21 shillings = £143.

ebts and Troubles

The Privy Council clamped down on broggers and suspended licensed wool-dealing. John Shakespeare fell into debt and mortgaged some of his property. He stopped attending Anglican services, claiming to be afraid of meeting creditors – and he may also have declared his faith as a Catholic. His application to the Heralds' College for a coat of arms was rejected, and he was eventually expelled from the Stratford council for absenteeism.

YET THROUGH THIS HE REMAINED "A MERRY CHEEKD OLD MAN", WORKING IN HIS SHOP, FATHERING MORE SHAKESPEARES AND JESTING WITH HIS SON.

Will was by now attending the local grammar school and doing his bit to maintain the family honour.

School Days

Then the whining schoolboy, with his satchel
And shining morning face, creeping like snail
Unwillingly to school.

As You Like It, II.vii.145-7

In Elizabethan England, the grammar school day ran from 6:00 in the morning until 5:30 in the afternoon, six days a week. Lessons were spent learning Latin, translating to and from Latin, and memorizing and reciting Latin poetry and prose.

ZZ
ZZZ

BY THE TIME BOYS REACHED THE UPPER CLASSES, IT WAS FORBIDDEN TO SPEAK ENGLISH IN SCHOOL.

Will spent probably eight years studying Latin, covering grammar, logic, rhetoric, the drama of Terence and Plautus, Virgil, and Ovid's *Metamorphoses*, a favourite.

His friend the playwright Ben Jonson later jested that Shakespeare had only "smalle Latine and lesse Greeke", but Latin poetry and rhetoric trained his ear and shaped his imagination. For his early tragedy, *Titus Andronicus*, Will was inspired by Ovid, Seneca and the Roman historians.

He continued to use Ovid's *Metamorphoses* (in Arthur Golding's translation) for inspiration throughout his writing career, checking it against the original Latin.

ost Years

Will may then have spent another two years teaching Latin as a schoolmaster for the Hoghton family in Lancashire. These are Shakespeare's "lost years". There is no reliable record of his activities, although the scholarly detail in his early plays might suggest a brief teaching placement. Many academics (being teachers themselves) support this theory, but there are others.

The wit and diplomat Duff Cooper wrote a book just after the war called *Sergeant Shakespeare* (1949) …

… ABOUT MY SUPPOSED LIFE IN THE ARMY.

The canoeist William Bliss imagined that Shakespeare circumnavigated the world with Sir Francis Drake …

… BEFORE BEING SHIPWRECKED ON A LATER VOYAGE.

Shakespeare's life has many blank passages in it, in which critics and biographers are liable to see their own reflections as clearly as they can – or not, as Anthony Burgess wrote in his biography of Shakespeare …

There are studies presenting Shakespeare as a Catholic, a Puritan, a Royalist, a Republican, etc., etc., but there is no firm evidence for these beliefs, just lines taken from the characters who speak in his plays. Shakespeare's own faith and politics are not evident from his writing.

# Marriage

We do know that Will Shakespeare married Anne Hathaway in late 1582. This union has provoked much biographical speculation. She was eight or nine years older than he was, and also three months pregnant. A predatory older woman? Or did Shakespeare woo her with his poems? His Sonnet 145 ends with a pun on her name, "Hathaway" …

"I hate" from hate away she threw, And sav'd my life, saying "not you."

The newly-weds moved in with the Shakespeare family at Henley Street, where Will probably helped out his father whose trade was now declining. Perhaps he worked as a part-time professional scribe as well.

OUR DAUGHTER SUSANNA WAS BORN IN MAY.

THREE YEARS LATER, STILL IN THE CROWDED FAMILY HOUSE, WE HAD TWINS – HAMNET AND JUDITH.

SHORTLY THEREAFTER, WILL LEFT FOR LONDON TO WORK IN THE THEATRE.

Although he regularly returned to Stratford and invested his money there, he had effectively abandoned his young family for a precarious career.

he Hireling Actor

Shakespeare probably began working as a hireling actor, taking whatever small roles were available.

He "did act exceedingly well", according to the literary historian **John Aubrey** (1626-97), and played in Ben Jonson's *Every Man in His Humour* (1598) and *Sejanus His Fall* (1603).

Shakespeare also acted in his own plays. There is a story of his brother …

"… having once seen him act a part in one of his own comedies, wherein being to personate a decrepit old man, he wore a long beard, and appeared so weak and drooping and unable to walk, that he was forced to be supported and carried by another person to a table, at which he was seated among company, who were eating, and one of them sung a song."

This is the part of Adam in *As You Like It*, II.iii.47-51.

*Though I look old,
yet I am strong and lusty;
For in my youth
I never did apply
Hot and rebellious
liquors in my blood,
Nor did not with
unbashful forehead woo
The means of
wickedness and debility.*

He also reputedly played the Ghost in *Hamlet*, I.v.15-20.

I could a tale unfold whose lightest word
Would harrow up thy soul, freeze thy young blood,
Make thy two eyes like stars start from their spheres,
Thy knotted and combined locks to part,
And each particular hair to stand an end,
Like quills upon the fearful porpentine.

The Influence of Acting on Writing

Shakespeare might also (according to recent computer analysis) have played the First Player in *Hamlet*, the black character Aaron in *Titus Andronicus*, Duke Theseus in *A Midsummer Night's Dream*, Antonio in *Twelfth Night*, even Ulysses in *Troilus and Cressida*, as well as miscellaneous kings, old men and choruses – such as Friar Laurence and the chorus in *Romeo and Juliet*, and old John of Gaunt and the Gardener in *Richard II*.

SHORT PARTS THAT WOULD USUALLY HAVE ME ON AND OFF IN EARLY SCENES – SOMETIMES WITH THE FIRST LINE – AND DELIVERING FINE SET-PIECE SPEECHES.

THE PARTS HE MEMORIZED FOR ONE PERFORMANCE, WHILE HE WAS COMPOSING A NEW PLAY, COULD ALSO HAVE INFLUENCED HIS WRITING STYLE.

His plays are in any case often linked. *A Midsummer Night's Dream*, possibly staged a few days after *Romeo and Juliet*, is a sharp parody of the earlier romantic tragedy. Shakespeare often alluded to his earlier works – and often ironically.

The Romantic poet **Samuel Taylor Coleridge** (1772-1834) later said …

"Great dramatists make great actors. But looking at him merely as a performer, I am certain he was greater as Adam, *in 'As you Like it,' than* Burbage, *as* Hamlet, *or* Richard the Third. *Think of the scene between him and* Orlando; *and think again, that the actor of that part had to carry the author of that play in his arms!*
Think of having had Shakespeare in one's arms! It is worth having died two hundred years ago to have heard Shakespeare deliver a single line. He must have been a great actor."

The Hireling Playwright

He had been writing poetry, and he began writing plays. His first might have been *The Two Gentlemen of Verona*, or an early version of *Hamlet*. He possibly wrote the first two acts of *Edward III* and collaborated on *The Book of Sir Thomas More* (adapted by Anthony Munday). The manuscript of *Sir Thomas More* survives. It is written in six different hands. The three folio pages of "Hand D" were identified in 1916 as being by Shakespeare.

IF THIS IS SO, THEY ARE THE ONLY SCENES WE HAVE IN SHAKESPEARE'S OWN HANDWRITING.

All the other play manuscripts and letters and notebooks have been lost. All that remain are a few signatures on legal documents.

Shakespeare's scene in *Sir Thomas More* is rapidly composed, barely punctuated, and extravagantly spelt (the name "More" is spelt in three different ways) – but it has a vivacious dramatic energy, as when More attempts to quell the clamorous crowd (*Sir Thomas More*, Addition II, 82-7).

> ... by this pattern
> Not one of you should live an aged man,
> For other ruffians, as their fancies wrought,
> With self-same hand, self reasons, and self right,
> Would shark on you, and men like ravenous fishes
> Would feed on one another.

The play was considered seditious and probably not performed. These pages show that Shakespeare was a fluent writer, a reviser of his own and others' work, a collaborator, an editor. In other words, Shakespeare's early career was as a *pen for hire*.

Elizabethan Theatre Work

Theatre work was collaborative, and not only during one's apprenticeship. Writing for the Elizabethan stage was teamwork, as was production and performance, and subsequent revision and publication. Shakespeare was a professional man of the theatre: an actor, a dramatist, and eventually a business partner. By writing for specific members of his company, such as the comedian Will Kemp, his work was very much the product of a specific moment in the history of drama.

ondon Life

We know very little of Shakespeare's life in London or anywhere. John Aubrey said he was "the more to be admired q [*quia*: because] he was not a company keeper lived in Shoreditch, wouldnt be debauched, & if invited to writ; [that] he was in paine". John Manningham, an Elizabethan law student, noted an anecdote about Shakespeare's sexual exploits in his diary for 1602. After playing the title in *Richard III*, Richard Burbage (Shakespeare's leading actor, 1567-1619) was met by a young lady and arranged to visit her at her lodgings, using the codename "Richard III".

> *I* OVERHEARD THESE ARRANGEMENTS, WENT EARLY TO THE LADY'S HOUSE, AND DECLARED MYSELF "*RICHARD III*".

He seduced her with his fine phrases and was "at his game" before Burbage arrived.

> *W*HEN BURBAGE APPEARED AND SAID THAT "*RICHARD III*" WAS NOW AT THE DOOR, SHAKESPEARE SENT DOWN A MESSAGE THAT *WILLIAM THE CONQUEROR* HAD COME BEFORE *RICHARD III*.

Shakespeare's Facility of Expression

Ben Jonson (1572/3-1637) clearly enjoyed Shakespeare's company …

"I lov'd the man, and doe honour his memory (on this side Idolatry) as much as any. Hee was (indeed) honest, and of an open, and free nature: had an excellent Phantsie; *brave notions, and gentle expressions: wherein hee flow'd with that facility that sometime it was necessary he should be stop'd … His wit was in his owne power; would the rule of it had beene so too. Many times hee fell into those things, could not escape laughter."*

The criticism that he overwrote is endorsed by the editors of the Oxford edition (1988) of Shakespeare's works who have compared different printed versions of the plays. The shorter texts are revised texts, closer to the plays as acted, and have cut certain

Shakespeare's English History

He was writing with increasing success and was fascinated by English history. Shakespeare was very interested in developing a national myth, and persistently returned to Raphael Holinshed's *Chronicles of England, Scotlande and Irelande* (1577) throughout his career.

> *I* WROTE MORE ABOUT ENGLISH HISTORY AND THE FORMATION OF *BRITAIN* THAN ANY OF MY CONTEMPORARIES IN THE THEATRE.

He was also interested in British ethnicities (Welsh, Scots, Irish), racial difference (Shylock, Othello, Caliban), and the lower classes – whether metropolitan (at Gad's Hill in *Henry IV*) or rustic (*The Winter's Tale*).

enry VI

The three parts of *Henry VI* must have been written sometime before 1592. They stemmed from an original two-part play by Shakespeare: *The First Part of the Contention betwixt the Two Famous Houses of York and Lancaste*r (published in 1594) and *The True Tragedy of Richard Duke of York* (1595). These became the second and third parts of what we now call *Henry VI*, and *Part One* was added later to complete the reign.

UNDER THE TITLE HARRY THE SIXTH IT PROVED A RUNAWAY SUCCESS AT PHILIP HENSLOWE'S ROSE THEATRE.

THEN THE PLAGUE WAS BACK AND THE THEATRES CLOSED.

The Hireling Poet

Shakespeare now briefly turned his ambitions to poetry and patronage, and wrote two erotic verses: *Venus and Adonis* (1593) and *The Rape of Lucrece* (1594). These are the only works he took any care in publishing, and they are effusively dedicated to Henry Wriothesley, third Earl of Southampton.

"The loue I dedicate to your Lordship is without end: wherof this Pamphlet without beginning is but a superfluous Moity. The warrant I haue of your Honourable disposition, not the worth of my vntutord Lines makes it assured of acceptance. What I haue done is yours, what I haue to doe is yours, being part in all I haue, deuoted yours. Were my worth greater, my duety would shew greater, meane time, as it is, it is bound to your Lordship; To whom I wish long life still lengthned with all happiness."

(Dedicatory letter, *The Rape of Lucrece*)

The Spelling of "Shak(e)speare"

Ironically, by a printer's accident these books also give us our spelling of Shakespeare's name. In his signatures, he is always *Shakspere* or *Shakspeare*, but because of the difficulty in printing the letters *k* and ∫ (the long *s*) next to each other, the dedications to Southampton are signed "William Shakespeare". This spelling has been conventional since the end of the 18th century.

BUT ELIZABETHAN SPELLING WAS ANYWAY VERY FLUID. AMONG THE 83 WAYS OF SPELLING MY NAME ARE ...

SHAKESPUR, SHAKESPERT, SHAKESBY, SHAKISPERE, SHAKYSPER, SHACKSPEER, SCHAKESPEYR, SCHACOSPER, SHAXBERD, SHAXVER, SHAXBEE, SHEXSPER, SAXPER, SHAGSPERE, SHASPER, SASHPIERRE, SADSPERE, SHAFFTESPERE, CHACSPER ...

n Upstart Crow

Shakespeare (however you spelt it) was gaining attention and notoriety. As an aspiring professional writer, he was unusual in the 1590s for not having attended university. In later years this relative lack of education became mythologized and implied that Shakespeare was a natural, unfettered genius. But at the time, some of his fellow writers thought he was simply a charlatan. **Robert Greene** (1558-92) made an explicit if contorted attack on Shakespeare in his *Groatsworth of Witte*, published posthumously in 1592 ...

"... there is an vpstart Crow, beautified with our feathers, that with his Tygers hart wrapt in a Players hyde, *supposes he is as well able to bombast out a blanke verse as the best of you: and beeing an absolute* Iohannes fac totum, *is in his owne conceit the onely Shake-scene in a countrey."*

Greene suggests that Shakespeare is a vicious plagiarist and rural bumpkin (the "Tygers hart" line is from *Henry VI Part Three*, I.iv.138).

it Marlowe

Among the university writers or "wits" there was one in particular who cast an immense shadow over the London theatre: **Christopher Marlowe** (1564-93). Marlowe was a poet, a playwright, and a polemicist.

HE DECLARED HIS ATHEISM ...

ALL PROTESTANTES ARE HYPO-CRITICAL ASSES ...

AND HIS TASTE FOR SMOKING AND PEDERASTY

ALL THEI THAT LOVE NOT TOBACCO AND BOIES ARE FOOLES.

ALTHOUGH HE WAS EXACTLY SHAKESPEARE'S AGE, KIT MARLOWE WAS ALREADY THE LEADING PLAY-WRIGHT OF HIS TIME.

Shakespeare was heavily influenced by Marlowe (he even quotes Marlowe's poem *Hero and Leander* in *As You Like It*), and this anxiety pervades several of his plays, which are in dialogue with Marlowe's body of work: imitating, parodying, rewriting, and ultimately overcoming his plays – right up to the end of his career.

But Shakespeare had two main advantages over Marlowe. Shakespeare was an actor, and therefore had a richer feeling for character. Marlowe had no such experience. This enabled Shakespeare to create characters as rich as Falstaff and shake off Marlowe's influence. The other advantage was that by then Marlowe was dead anyway: murdered by Ingram Friser, Robert Poley and Nicholas Skeres in a "small room" at Deptford on 30 May 1593.

So Shakespeare's attempts to get the Earl of Southampton to patronize his poetry looked premature after the publication of *Lucrece* in 1594. The plague was subsiding, but the theatres now looked denuded. The older generation of Greene and Peele was rapidly passing away and there was no one else to take over after Marlowe's shocking end. Shakespeare returned to the theatre and recommenced his dramatic career with a flourish. In the 16th century, plays might be performed as part of an ongoing repertoire, being repeated every week or so while they continued to attract audiences.

SHAKESPEARE'S *TITUS ANDRONICUS* WAS A TERRIFIC HIT ...

IN *1594* IT WAS ONCE PERFORMED THREE TIMES IN SIX DAYS AT THE *ROSE THEATRE* - QUITE A FEAT, AS THE AVERAGE LIFE OF A PLAY WAS A MERE DOZEN PERFORMANCES OVER A FEW MONTHS.

10

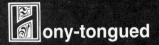

Hony-tongued

Shakespeare was writing on average two plays a year. By 1598, Francis Meres could write in his contemporary compendium *Palladis Tamia* that "the sweete wittie soule of Ouid liues in mellifluous & hony-tongued *Shakespeare*, witnes his *Venus* and *Adonis*, his *Lucrece*, his sugred Sonnets among his priuate friends, &c". Meres goes on …

PLAUTUS

SENECA

As Plautus *and* Seneca *are accounted the best for Comedy and Tragedy among the Latines: so* Shakespeare *among the English is the most excellent in both kinds for the stage; for Comedy, witnes his* Gentlemen of Verona, *his* Errors, *his* Loue labors lost, *his* Loue labors wonne, *his* Midsummers night dreame, *& his* Merchant of Venice: *for Tragedy his* Richard the 2. Richard the 3. Henry the 4. King Iohn, Titus Andronicus *and his* Romeo and Juliet.

haxpier Gains Success

Meres reports on a good start. Indeed, *Henry IV Part One,* which introduced Falstaff, was one of the most popular plays of the time. First published in 1598, it was reprinted more often in Shakespeare's lifetime than any other of his plays. But read the list again and notice *Love's Labour's Won.*

ublished Plays

Despite the success of their resident playwright, Shakespeare's company (called the Chamberlain's Men) were in dire financial straits by 1597 and had to sell off the playbooks of *Love's Labour's Lost* and *Richard II* in 1598 and *Henry IV Part One* and *Richard III* in 1599. About half of Shakespeare's plays were printed in such individual "Quarto" copies (Quarto refers to the size of the book) before the big "Folio" of 36 plays was published posthumously in 1623.

This may have been in part deliberate. It was a desperate act for the company to lose its monopoly on performances, although such sales did create a reading audience for the plays.

Comparing the Bad Quarto of *Hamlet*

In all, six or seven of Shakespeare's Quartos (*Henry VI Parts Two* and *Three, Romeo and Juliet, Henry V, The Merry Wives of Windsor, Hamlet* and possibly *Love's Labour's Lost*) originally appeared as "bad" Quartos: the texts being based on actors' memories or even shorthand notes taken during a performance. The Shakespeare scholar E.K. Chambers notes of the "reporter" who cribbed the "bad" Quarto of *Hamlet* (1603) …

HE MAKES OMISSIONS, CAUSING LACUNAE OF SENSE AND GRAMMAR. HE GIVES THE BEGINNINGS AND ENDS OF SPEECHES WITHOUT THEIR MIDDLES. HE PARAPHRASES. HE MERGES DISTINCT SPEECHES. HE MAKES A MOSAIC OF RECOLLECTED FRAGMENTS. HE CATCHES VIGOROUS WORDS WITHOUT THEIR CONTEXT. HE MAKES DOUBLE USE OF PHRASES. HE SHIFTS THE ORDER OF BITS OF DIALOGUE WITHIN THEIR SCENES …

And he comes out with speeches such as this ...

To be, or not to be, I there's the point,
To Die, to sleepe, is that all? I all:
No, to sleepe, to dreame, I mary there it goes,
For in that dreame of death, when wee awake,
And borne before an euerlasting Iudge,
From whence no passenger euer retur'ned,
The vndiscouered country, at whose sight
The happy smile, and the accursed damn'd.
But for this, the ioyfull hope of this,
Who'ld beare the scorns and flattery of the world,
Scorned by the right rich, the rich curssed of the poore?

Very different from the now commonly accepted speech ...

To be, or not to be: that is the question:
Whether 'tis nobler in the mind to suffer
The slings and arrows of outrageous fortune,
Or to take arms against a sea of troubles,
And by opposing end them? To die: to sleep;
No more; and, by a sleep to say we end
The heart-ache and the thousand natural shocks
That flesh is heir to, 'tis a consummation
Devoutly to be wish'd. To die, to sleep;
To sleep: perchance to dream: ay, there's the rub;
For in that sleep of death what dreams may come
When we have shuffled off this mortal coil,
Must give us pause. [...]
But that the dread of something after death,
The undiscover'd country from whose bourn
No traveller returns, puzzles the will,
And makes us rather bear those ills we have,
Than fly to others that we know not of [...]

amlet's Revision

The bad Quartos are useful, however, because they demonstrate theatre practice – for example, the extent in which plays were cut and revised. This is of course part of the action in *Hamlet*. The Prince turns *The Murder of Gonzago* into *The Mousetrap*, a "play within a play", by inserting 12-16 lines of his own composing.

WHAT DO YOU CALL THE PLAY?

THE MOUSETRAP. ...THIS PLAY IS THE IMAGE OF A MURDER DONE IN VIENNA.

The other eight Quartos we have of Shakespearean plays are "good" Quartos, which means that they were authorized by Shakespeare and the players: *Titus Andronicus, Richard II, Richard III, Henry IV Parts One* and *Two, Much Ado About Nothing, A Midsummer Night's Dream,* and *The Merchant of Venice*.

The Chamberlain's Men now left the Rose and built the Globe Theatre. It opened with *Julius Caesar* in 1599. Shakespeare followed this with *Hamlet*, and then *Troilus and Cressida* (which was performed neither then, nor for almost three centuries). Nevertheless, with *Hamlet*, Shakespeare had moved into another realm. Gabriel Harvey said in about 1601 …

THE YOUNGER SORT TAKES MUCH DELIGHT IN SHAKESPEARES VENUS, & ADONIS: BUT HIS LUCRECE, & HIS TRAGEDIE OF HAMLET, PRINCE OF DENMARKE, HAVE IT IN THEM, TO PLEASE THE WISER SORT.

 # "Personal" *Hamlet*?

The immense capacity of *Hamlet*, its copiousness and fertility and
exuberance, not to mention its psychological intensity, tempts critics to
personalize the play. Shakespeare's only son, Hamnet (Hamnet and
Hamlet were variations of the same name) died in 1596, aged only
eleven.

The play not only adapts
literary sources but also
capitalizes on Shakespeare's own
life and Stratford upbringing.

In 1597, Shakespeare renewed his commitment to Stratford and bought New Place or "The Great House", the second largest house in the town.

... AN ENORMOUS DWELLING WITH TWO GARDENS, TWO BARNS, AND TEN FIREPLACES.

It would be Shakespeare's home until he died. He had also recently acquired his coat of arms (which were gratifyingly bestowed upon his father). So family concerns were uppermost in his mind.

The Original or *"Ur-Hamlet"*

On the other hand, contemporary thinking is that Shakespeare adapted an earlier play, the *"Ur-Hamlet"*, played at least as early as 1594 and perhaps dating from the 1580s. The critic Harold Bloom argues persuasively that the *Ur-Hamlet* is in fact Shakespeare's first, lost play, dating from 1588 and soon after adapted by Thomas Kyd as *The Spanish Tragedy*.

SHAKESPEARE REWROTE *HAMLET* ALMOST PERPETUALLY ...

I WAS ALSO WRITING OTHER THINGS TOO, OF COURSE.

The joyous *As You Like It*, for example, was probably written in 1599. This discourages seeing the melancholy *Hamlet* as a symptom of depression.

Shakespeare also became briefly involved in political dissent at this time. His two series of English history plays included the deposition of two monarchs (Richard II and Richard III). There were contemporary problems with the play *Richard II* because of its comparisons with Elizabeth I.

On 7 February 1601, the afternoon before they attempted a *coup d'état*, a group led by the Earl of Essex sponsored a performance of *Richard II* by the Chamberlain's Men.

Changing Fortunes

The Essex rebellion failed. Shakespeare's actors were taken in for questioning but escaped prosecution.

Of course, on the eventual ascension of James VI, Shakespeare's company received a minor acknowledgement: they became the King's Men, and were effectively recognized as the leading

With that, Shakespeare's rate of production now halved from two plays to one play a year. He lodged in St Helen's in London, possibly sharing a tenement with a musician, Thomas Morley, and was surrounded by *emigré* families from France and the Lowlands.

Later, when relations between the two families soured, Shakespeare was obliged to make a legal deposition describing the events (1612). In 1608, Shakespeare became a shareholder in the Blackfriars Theatre, a roofed performance space, and as late as 1615, he was defending his rights on this property.

etirement

There is a myth that *The Tempest* is Shakespeare's farewell to the stage, even that it is an allegory of his whole life. The poet **Robert Graves** (1895-1985) announced that "tradition has always identified Prospero with Shakespeare himself". This is inevitable. Prospero, as an artist and illusionist, can be identified with a poet in dozens of ways. But in fact Shakespeare wrote another three plays with **John Fletcher** (1579-1625), his successor at Blackfriars, after *The Tempest: The Two Noble Kinsmen*, *Cardenio* (lost), and *Henry VIII* (or *All is True*).

> IT WAS A PERFORMANCE OF *HENRY VIII*, WHICH INVOLVED SOME GUNPOWDER SPECIAL EFFECTS, THAT IGNITED THE *GLOBE* THEATRE AND BURNT IT DOWN IN *1613*.

It was immediately rebuilt and continued to stage plays until it was closed down at the start of the English Civil War in 1642. Two years later it was demolished – in order to build cheap housing …

Shakespeare retired to Stratford and apparently abandoned writing. The only text from this final period is his will, which has provoked much speculation because of the strange bequest to Anne, his wife. Between two lines is added: *"Item, I give to my wife my second-best bed with furniture"*. This is the only mention of her in the entire document. Is it a deliberate snub and contrived to deny her control of any element of his estate?

So, is this simply a conventional way of expressing affection? The will also includes elaborate instructions for keeping Shakespeare's male line alive through his daughter Susanna's son – although in the event she never had a son and so the direct line was extinct by 1670. The will was also revised to provide for his daughter Judith, who had just married a ne'er-do-well named Thomas Quiney.

eath

Less than a month after probating this document, Shakespeare died on 23 April 1616, aged 52. Evidently he had a fever, possibly typhoid. According to a Stratford doctor, this had been contracted when …

Shakespeare is buried "full seventeen foot deep, deep enough to secure him" (according to a visitor 78 years later) in Holy Trinity Church, Stratford. It is claimed, of course, that he wrote his epitaph himself …

GOOD FREND FOR
IESVS SAKE FORBEARE,
TO DIGG THE DVST
ENCLOASED HEARE!
BLESSED BE YE MAN YT
SPARES THES STONES,
AND CVRST BE HE YT
MOVES MY BONES.

The current stone is in fact a copy of the original which was replaced in the middle of the 18th century.

PROBABLY ONLY A SIXTH OF ALL THE PLAYS WRITTEN BY ENGLISH PLAYWRIGHTS BETWEEN 1560 AND 1642 SURVIVE.

SHAKESPEARE'S PLAYS SURVIVED BECAUSE HE WAS ENORMOUSLY POPULAR, BUT ALSO BECAUSE HE WAS LUCKY.

IT IS THAT LUCK THAT HAS EXERCISED CERTAIN CULTURAL COMMENTATORS EVER SINCE.

Early Myths of Shakespeare's Life

The scant details of Shakespeare's life were soon enhanced by myths. It was believed that John Shakespeare was a butcher, which led to the rumour of Will learning how to slaughter: "When he kill'd a calf, he would doe it in a high style, and make a speech". This eco-friendly Shakespeare develops into a Robin Hood figure in a tale about poaching deer from one Sir Thomas Lucy, by whom he was prosecuted (and possibly whipped).

I RESPONDED BY NAILING UP A SCURRILOUS BALLAD ABOUT "*LOUSY LUCY*" THAT FORCED THE LANDOWNER TO LEAVE THE COUNTY FOR A WHILE.

VERSIONS OF THIS BALLAD TURNED UP THROUGHOUT THE *18*TH CENTURY, UNTIL IT WAS QUERIED WHETHER *SIR THOMAS LUCY* EVER POSSESSED A DEER PARK.

Against the troubled background of the French Revolution, even this minor attack on the aristocracy was declared false. But the anecdote may nevertheless contain a grain of truth.

Shakespeare the Entrepreneur

When the theatres reopened after the Restoration of Charles II in 1660, a playwright named **William Davenant** (1606-68) led the company of the Duke's Men. Shakespeare was William Davenant's god-father.

Davenant's story gained credence in the 18th century and led to a legend that Shakespeare had been so successful at this work that he organized a group of lads called "Shakespeare's Boys" – a fitting fable of entrepreneurship for the times.

51

Gentrified Shakespeare

Likewise, **Alexander Pope** (1688-1744), in *The First Epistle of the Second Book of Horace, Imitated* (1737), justifies poetic fame and fortune in an image of Shakespeare as a literary entrepreneur and theatrical impresario ...

> *Shakespear, (whom you and ev'ry Play-house bill*
> *Style the divine, the matchless, what you will)*
> *For gain, not glory, wing'd his roving flight,*
> *And grew Immortal in his own despight.*

Consequently, his admirers craved any physical connection they could find with the writer – any *commodities*.

The Bard's Relics

Before he left Stratford, Shakespeare had supposedly slept beneath a crab-apple tree ("Shakespeare's Canopy") following a drinking contest with some men from neighbouring Bidford. The tree was torn to pieces by souvenir hunters. Among relics of the Bard held at Stratford were his pencil case, walking stick, two pairs of gloves, shoe-horn, brooch, ring, table, spoon, salt-cellar, half-pint mug, ink-stand, clock, shovel-board, chair and bench.

HIS CHAIR GRADUALLY DISAPPEARED AS SOUVENIR SLICES WERE CUT FROM IT, UNTIL IT WAS PURCHASED BY A POLISH PRINCESS AT THE END OF THE *18TH* CENTURY.

The Stratford tourist trade was clearly benefiting. In 1769, the actor **David Garrick** (1717-79) organized the first Shakespeare jubilee there. Later, after the railway had come to Stratford in 1860, some 30,000 tourists were able to attend the 1864 tricentennial jubilee. Festivals became annual shortly thereafter.

Manuscripts and Shakespeare's Books

There were no Shakespeare manuscripts. According to an improbable report of 1729 ...

Two *large* Chests *full of this GREAT MAN'S* loose Papers *and* Manuscripts, *in the Hands of an ignorant* Baker *of WARWICK, (who married one of the Descendants from* Shakespear*) were carelessly scatter'd and thrown about, as Garrett Lumber and Litter, to the particular Knowledge of the late Sir William Bishop, till they were all consum'd in the generall Fire and Destruction of that Town.*

And somewhere there were supposed to be his books: signed copies of Bacon's *Essays*, Florio's Montaigne, a prayer book and a map of Cambridge presented by Ben Jonson. The eventual consequence of these legends, of course, was that manuscripts were forged. One of the most notorious forgers was **William Henry Ireland** (1775-1835) who presented legal documents, letters and love poems (enclosing a lock of Shakespeare's hair), a manuscript of *King Lear* and two new plays: *Vortigern* and *Henry II*.

VORTIGERN WAS PERFORMED IN *1796* ...

BUT BEFORE THE PLAY WAS ENDED, THE HOUSE WAS IN UPROAR!

More subtle were **John Payne Collier**'s forgeries. Collier (1789-1883) fabricated supplementary historical material, and eventually annotations in a copy of the Second Folio that had supposedly belonged to Thomas Perkins, a colleague of Shakespeare's who had corrected the text.

The most renowned relic was the mulberry tree ostensibly planted by Shakespeare in his garden at New Place. But this was chopped down by the Reverend Francis Gastrell, shortly before he demolished the entire house — much to the dismay of Bardolaters.

ALTHOUGH THE BUILDING HAD ALREADY BEEN REBUILT ONCE.

A local carpenter bought the mulberry timber.

I SPENT THE REST OF MY LIFE CARVING SOUVENIR MEMENTOS AND KNICK-KNACKS FROM THE WOOD.

Nevertheless, Shakespeare's birthplace was still standing. In 1847, the novelist Charles Dickens and the actor William Macready led a campaign to prevent the Amercan circus impresario **P.T. Barnum** (1810-91) from purchasing the site.

P.T.BARNUM
CIRCUS

WE SET UP A PUBLIC SUBSCRIPTION AND ACQUIRED IT FOR THE NATION.

Shakespeare's desk was still being displayed to visitors at the school in the late 19th century. There was even a story of a dog, "spoted like a leper", supposedly descended from Shakespeare's coach dog.

atural Genius

Shakespeare was considered to be a natural, untutored genius, despite the evidence that he read extensively for each play, took pains over rewriting and revised the text in rehearsal – which is evident from comparing Quarto versions of plays with those printed in the Folio. Ben Jonson described Shakespeare as an unlearned but naturally gifted writer.

Jonson praised Shakespeare for precisely this labour in his eulogy …

For though the Poets *matter, Nature be,*
His art doth giue the fashion. And, that he,
Who casts to write a liuing line, must sweat,
(such as thine are) and strike the second heat
Vpon the Muses *anuile: turne the same,*
(And himselfe with it) that he thinkes to frame;
Or for the lawrell, he may gaine a scorne …

WE CAN AGREE THAT SHAKESPEARE DID GIVE A "LIVELY TURN" TO FAMILIAR MATERIAL …

FOR A GOOD POET'S MADE, AS WELL AS BORN. AND SUCH WERT THOU.

Indeed, though very good at handling plot, Shakespeare was not particularly good at inventing it, whether in the early *Merry Wives of Windsor* (lightly based on Ovid), or later in *The Tempest*, although perhaps his two most personal plays – *Love's Labour's Lost* and *A Midsummer Night's Dream* – were original plots. He generally took stories from sources familiar in his time – Holinshed's *Chronicles*, North's translation of Plutarch's *Parallel Lives of the Greeks and Romans*, Chapman's translation of Homer, Holland's Pliny, Florio's Montaigne and Golding's Ovid.

I SHALL RENDER THIS ...

The barge she sat in, like a burnish'd throne,
Burnt on the water. The poop was beaten gold,
Purple the sails, and so perfumed that
The winds were love-sick with them; the oars were silver,
Which to the tune of flutes kept stroke, and made
The water which they beat to follow faster,
As amorous of their strokes ...

AND IT IS WORTH NOTING THAT *T.S. ELIOT* (1888-1965) KEEPS UP THE TRADITION IN *THE WASTE LAND, ll.77-8*, (1922), BORROWING FROM *ANTONY AND CLEOPATRA, ll.ll.191-7.*

THE CHAIR SHE SAT IN, LIKE A BURNISHED THRONE, GLOWED ON THE MARBLE ...

"By the dim light of Nature"

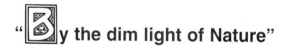

Shakespeare-the-natural-genius was a myth already popular during his lifetime. **Francis Beaumont** (1584-1616) in *The Knight of the Burning Pestle* (1607-8) wrote ...

> And from all learning keep these lines as clear
> As Shakespeare's best are, which our heirs shall hear
> Preachers apt to their auditors to show
> How far sometimes a mortal man may go
> By the dim light of Nature.

Shortly after Shakespeare's death, **John Milton** (1608-74) wrote in "L'Allegro" of hearing ...

... sweetest Shakespeare fancy's child,
Warble his native wood-notes wild.

Later still, Samuel Taylor Coleridge concurred …

Shakspeare, no mere child of nature; no automaton of genius; no passive vehicle of inspiration possessed by the spirit, not possessing it; first studied patiently, meditated deeply, understood minutely, till knowledge, become habitual and intuitive, wedding itself to his habitual feelings, and at length gave birth to that stupendous power, by which he stands alone, with no equal or second in his own class; to that power which seated him on one of the two glory-smitten summits of the poetic mountain, with Milton as his compeer not rival.

NEVERTHELESS, IN TRULY ROMANTIC FASHION, HE GOES ON TO EMPHASIZE …

HE WAS THAT CHILD OF NATURE, AND NOT THE CREATURE OF HIS OWN EFFORTS.

Peculiarly English Freedom

Shakespeare was possibly the first writer in Western high culture to be applauded for his apparent lack of artifice. This marks a profound break with the classical tradition in which it was the imitation of earlier writers that was the measure of greatness.
Neo-classicists objected to Shakespeare because …

But these features were also welcomed as an escape from classical norms into a new form of expression, **peculiarly English.**

Shakespeare offered an escape from classical tyranny and demonstrated the instinctive freedoms of the English constitution.

Gothic and Sublime Genius

He was Gothic and sublime. **Joseph Addison** (1672-1719) in *Spectator* 419 declared ...

Among the English, Shakespear has incomparably excelled all others. That noble Extravagance of Fancy which he had in so great Perfection, thoroughly qualified him to touch this weak superstitious Part of his Reader's Imagination; and made him capable of succeeding, where he had nothing to support him besides the Strength of his own Genius.

THE WORD "GENIUS" EFFECTIVELY BEGAN TO MEAN **SHAKESPEAREAN** – AND **ENGLISH** ...

... RICH AND FERTILE AND FREE – BUT NOT SO FOR **MR RYMER!**

IN THE **N**EIGHING OF AN **H**ORSE, OR IN THE GROWLING OF A **M**ASTIFF, THERE IS A MEANING, THERE IS AS LIVELY EXPRESSION, AND, MAY **I** SAY, MORE HUMANITY, THAN MANY TIMES IN THE **T**RAGICAL FLIGHTS OF **S**HAKESPEAR.

Thomas Rymer (1641-1713), the first professional English critic, attacked Shakespeare for his linguistic copiousness and abundance.

The Splendours of Shakespeare

Lewis Theobald (1688-1744), in the preface to his edition of Shakespeare's works, was dazzled …

THE attempt to write upon SHAKESPEARE is like going into a large, a spacious, and a splendid dome through the conveyance of a narrow and obscure entry.

A glare of light suddenly breaks upon you beyond what the avenue at first promised …

… and a thousand beauties of genius and character, like so many gaudy apartments pouring at once upon the eye, diffuse and throw themselves out to the mind.

The prospect is too wide to come within the compass of a single view …

Thomas De Quincey (1785-1859), in his eerie essay, "On the Knocking at the Gate in *Macbeth*", concludes in rapture …

O MIGHTY POET! *T*HY WORKS ARE NOT AS THOSE OF OTHER MEN, SIMPLY AND MERELY GREAT WORKS OF ART, BUT ARE ALSO LIKE THE PHENOMENA OF NATURE ...

… *like the sun and the sea, the stars and the flowers, like frost and snow, rain and dew, hailstorm and thunder, which are to be studied with entire submission of our own faculties … the farther we press in our discoveries, the more we shall see proofs of design and self-supporting arrangement where the careless eye had seen nothing but accident!*

The Rise of Shakespeare's Popularity

During the Restoration, Ben Jonson was actually more highly thought of, and more often quoted, than Shakespeare. But Jonson was considered a highbrow playwright.

SHAKESPEARE HAD THE POPULAR VOTE, ESPECIALLY THROUGH ADAPTATIONS OF HIS WORKS.

JOHN DRYDEN (1631-1700), WHO REWORKED ANTONY AND CLEOPATRA INTO ALL FOR LOVE (1678) ACKNOWLEDGED SHAKESPEARE'S CONSUMMATE GENIUS.

AND WITH THE RISE OF THE 18TH-CENTURY MIDDLE CLASSES, SHAKESPEARE WAS TAKEN UP BY THE TATLER MAGAZINE ...

... WHICH PERSISTENTLY QUOTED HIM.

William Smith's influential translation of Longinus' *On the Sublime* (1739) used frequent examples from Shakespeare. **Edward Young** (1683-1765), in *Conjectures on Original Composition* (1759), argued that Jonson …

18th-Century Editions

The editing of Shakespeare in the 18th century is a lesson in the construction of a cultural artefact. The Tonson publishing firm enjoyed a virtual monopoly over the editing of Shakespeare. Tonson's played off editors against each other, choosing those who already had a literary reputation, and were antagonistic to their predecessors.

IN 1709, NICHOLAS ROWE (1674-1718), "A GENTLEMAN, WHO LOV'D TO LIE IN BED ALL DAY FOR HIS EASE, AND TO SIT UP ALL NIGHT FOR HIS PLEASURE", FIRST EDITED SHAKESPEARE FROM THE FOURTH FOLIO.

I WAS THE BEST TRAGEDIAN OF MY TIME, AND ALSO A SHAKESPEARE IMITATOR IN MY PLAY JANE SHORE (1714).

Rowe's edition was illustrated, had lists of dramatis personae that emphasized names rather than generic titles like "King", "Clowne" or "Bastard", and created minor characters by attributing various speeches and roles to one identity. Rowe also wrote the first

Rowe's success was followed in 1725 by the renowned poet Alexander Pope, whose edition laid emphasis on the best passages of Shakespeare's poetry for a reading audience.

I ASSUMED THAT SHAKESPEARE'S ACTORS HAD MANGLED THE TEXT AND THEREFORE I REWROTE IT.

POPE WAS FOLLOWED IN 1734 BY LEWIS THEOBALD, WHOSE FIRST TEXTUAL MONOGRAPH ON SHAKESPEARE HAD SAVAGED POPE'S EDITION.

FOR HIS PAINS, I CROWNED HIM "KING OF THE DUNCES" IN MY SATIRICAL EPIC THE DUNCIAD (1728).

ubsequent Tonson Editions

Theobald was the leading 16th-century scholar of his generation. His edition was followed in 1747 by that of **William Warburton** (1698-1779). Warburton was Pope's literary executor.

MY EDITION WAS SOLD AS MUCH AS IF IT WERE A NEW EDITION OF POPE AS IT WAS OF SHAKESPEARE.

WILLIAM HAWKINS, PROFESSOR OF POETRY AT OXFORD, LECTURED ON SHAKESPEARE FOR THE FIRST TIME IN A BRITISH UNIVERSITY IN 1751-6 (THE LECTURES WERE PUBLISHED IN 1758).

IN 1765, SAMUEL JOHNSON (1709-84), DICTIONARY-MAKER, ALL-ROUND PROFESSIONAL WRITER AND LITERARY CLUBMAN, PUBLISHED HIS OWN TONSON EDITION.

IT WAS A COMPILATION OF WHAT ALL THE PREVIOUS EDITORS HAD SAID BEFORE ME.

Johnson's "variorum" was a runaway success and inspired the later editions of **George Steevens** (1736-1800) and **Edmond Malone** (1741-1812).

The Shakespeare Apocrypha

What did Shakespeare mean in the 18th century? William Winstanley in *The Lives of the Most Famous English Poets* (1687) catalogued no fewer than 48 plays by Shakespeare, including *Lord Thomas Cromwell, Locrine, The London Prodigal, Sir John Oldcastle, The Puritan or The Widow of Watling Street, The Yorkshire Tragedy* and *The Birth of Merlin*. (All but the last had been added to the Third Folio edition of 1663.)

MANY MORE APOCRYPHAL PLAYS WERE ASSIGNED TO SHAKESPEARE, INCLUDING ...

... *Fair Em, The Merry Devil of Edmonton, Arden of Faversham, The Reign of King Edward III, Mucedorus* and *The Second Maiden's Tragedy*. There were also apparently "lost" plays: *Love's Labour's Won*, possibly *Henry I* and *Henry II, King Stephen, Duke Humphrey, Iphis and Iantha,* and most compellingly, *Cardenio*.

Cardenio, or The Double Falsehood

Only *Cardenio* has any substance. The editor Lewis Theobald's play *The Double Falsehood*, performed in December 1727 and published in 1728, purported to be a new work by Shakespeare. It is conceivably a version of *Cardenio*. It is based on an episode from a 1612 translation of Cervantes' *Don Quixote* (1605-15) in a heavily revised version prepared for, but never performed on, the Restoration stage. It was re-edited by Theobald for 18th-century performance, though the manuscripts were subsequently lost. As the critic Jonathan Bate says, "Reading it, one hears the faint cry of a Shakespeare and Fletcher original trapped below the layers of rewriting …"

Cervantes

What you can say is most unseasonable; what sing,
Most absonant and harsh: nay, your perfume,
Which I smell hither, cheers not my sense
Like our field-violet's breath.

The Double Falsehood, I.iii.54-7

Lewis Theobald was too sensitive to the un-Shakespearean qualities of the play. He anticipated criticism in his preface by commenting that some might say ...

20th-century **stylometry**, which analyses dramatists in terms of the frequency of minor words, contractions, and patterns of usage and occurrence of rare words – for example, use of *thee* and *thou*, *ye* and *you*, *I'm*, and so forth – may yet solve the secret of *The Double Falsehood*.

18th-Century Miscellany

Samuel Johnson's *Dictionary* (1755-6), completed a good decade before his Tonson edition, was effectively his first major Shakespearean project, since he took examples predominantly from the Bard.

SHAKESPEARE, NOTABLE FOR HIS COINAGES AND NEOLOGISMS, NOW BECAME A TOUCHSTONE OF THE CORRECT USAGE OF THE ENGLISH LANGUAGE.

Oxford English Dictionary

The strategy was repeated by **James Murray** (1837-1915), editor of the 19th-century *New English Dictionary* (which we know today as the *Oxford English Dictionary*), which also cited Shakespeare more than any other writer.

Johnson positioned himself at the centre of a coterie of Shakespeareans who made teamwork the scholarly standard, emphasizing the immense poetic resources of Shakespeare. There was, for example, great interest in establishing the "intellectual credentials" of this untutored genius. This inspired **Richard Farmer** (1735-97), an indolent Fellow of Emmanuel, Cambridge, to write his *Essay on the Learning of Shakespeare* (1767) on the subject.

I LOVED OLD PORT, OLD CLOTHES AND OLD BOOKS, AND COULD NOT BE PERSUADED TO RISE IN THE MORNING, GO TO BED AT NIGHT, OR SETTLE AN ACCOUNT.

JOHNSON, ANOTHER MAN WHO STYLED HIMSELF AS "THE MOST INDOLENT IN THE KINGDOM" AND ONCE DICTATED A BOOK FROM HIS BED, SAID OF FARMER'S ESSAY ...

YOU HAVE DONE THAT WHICH NEVER WAS DONE BEFORE; THAT IS, YOU HAVE COMPLETELY FINISHED A CONTROVERSY BEYOND ALL FURTHER DOUBT.

Farmer decided that "*Shakespeare* wanted not the Stilts of Languages to raise him above all other men".

Preposterous Facts and Scholarly Scepticism

Meanwhile, 18th-century editing was not without its mischief. George Steevens, "the Puck of commentators", impishly attributed his elucidations of Shakespeare's bawdy to two strait-laced clergymen, and added preposterous footnotes to the text. For example, for *Twelfth Night,* I.iii.42, he glossed a "parish top" …

This is one of the old customs now laid aside. A large [spinning] *top was formerly kept in every village, to be whipped in frosty weather, that the peasants may be kept warm by exercise, and out of mischief, while they could not work.*

THE NOTE SURVIVES INTO THE CURRENT *RIVERSIDE* EDITION, FIRST PUBLISHED IN *1974* …!

Biographical Fact and Fiction

Shakespeare's first real biographer was his first proper editor, Nicholas Rowe, who wrote his biography in 1708 and prefaced it to his complete edition of the works in 1709. It became the standard life of Shakespeare for the 18th century. Edmond Malone was later to claim that there were no more than eleven biographical facts in it ...

EIGHT OF WHICH ARE WRONG AND ONE DUBIOUS, LEAVING ONLY SHAKESPEARE'S BAPTISM AND BURIAL.

MY ONE-TIME COLLABORATOR GEORGE STEEVENS WAS ALSO DEEPLY SCEPTICAL, AS HE PUT IT ...

As all that is known with any degree of certainty concerning Shakespeare is, – that he was born at Stratford upon Avon, – married and had children there, – went to London, where he commenced actor, and wrote poems and plays, – returned to Stratford, made his will, died, and was buried, – I must confess my readiness to combat every unfounded supposition respecting the particular occurrences of his life.

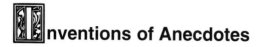nventions of Anecdotes

Steevens emphasizes official documentation and parish records – births, deaths and marriages – what one would expect from a legalistic Enlightenment scholar. But **William Oldys** (1696-1761) had already proposed that Shakespeare's birthday was St George's Day, and there were other traditions too. According to **William Guthrie** in 1747 …

SHAKESPEAR SHUT HIMSELF UP ALL NIGHT IN WESTMINSTER-ABBEY WHEN HE WROTE THE SCENE OF THE GHOST IN *HAMLET*.

HE ALSO SAYS THAT *I* WENT TO THE WHITE CLIFFS OF *DOVER* TO WRITE ACT *IV* OF *KING LEAR*.

Such colourful tales were difficult to ignore. Biography and memoir were growing in popularity, especially after James Boswell's *Life of Johnson* (1791), when biographical criticism became the critical orthodoxy. The problem with Shakespeare was not how little one knew, but how much could be *inferred* or simply *made up*.

CHARLES GILDON DISAGREED: THE GHOST SCENE WAS WRITTEN IN SHAKESPEARE'S HOUSE IN STRATFORD, ADJACENT TO THE CHARNEL HOUSE!

The Sonnets as Autobiography

So it was in the 18th century that Shakespeare's Sonnets began to be read as autobiographical, describing real people. The "Young Man" is usually supposed to have had a destructive affair with the "Dark Lady".

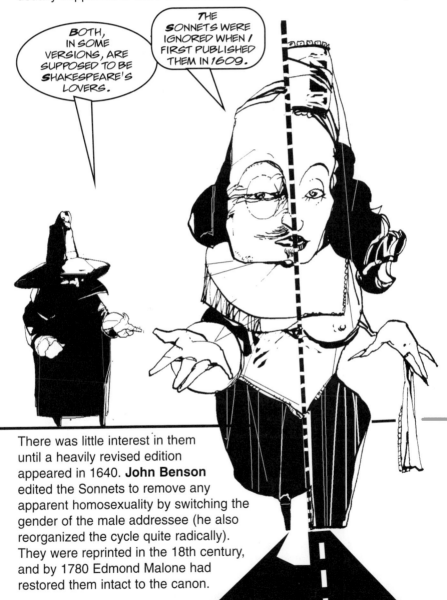

BOTH, IN SOME VERSIONS, ARE SUPPOSED TO BE SHAKESPEARE'S LOVERS.

THE SONNETS WERE IGNORED WHEN I FIRST PUBLISHED THEM IN 1609.

There was little interest in them until a heavily revised edition appeared in 1640. **John Benson** edited the Sonnets to remove any apparent homosexuality by switching the gender of the male addressee (he also reorganized the cycle quite radically). They were reprinted in the 18th century, and by 1780 Edmond Malone had restored them intact to the canon.

Shakespeare's "Confessions"?

William Wordsworth (1770-1850) later wrote his own sonnet on Shakespeare's Sonnets ...

Scorn not the Sonnet ...
            with this key
Shakespeare unlocked his heart

Robert Browning (1812-89) scoffed at Wordsworth forty years later, and he was correct. The Sonnets are flamboyant Renaissance examples of poetic and dramatic playfulness. But because comparatively little is known of Shakespeare himself, the temptation to read them autobiographically is almost irresistible.

August Wilhelm von Schlegel (1767-1845), the German translator of Shakespeare, outlined the emergent manifesto in a lecture in Vienna in 1808.

It betrays more than ordinary deficiency of critical acumen in Shakspeare's commentators that none of them, as far as we know, have ever thought of availing themselves of his sonnets for tracing the circumstances of his life. These sonnets paint most unequivocally the actual situation and sentiments of the poet; they make us acquainted with the passions of the man; they even contain remarkable confessions of his youthful errors.

INDEED THEY DO, AND ONE OF THE ODDITIES IN READING SHAKESPEARE'S SONNETS AS AUTOBIOGRAPHICAL IS THAT THEY GIVE HIM A **LIMP** ...

SONNET **37**: "SO I, MADE LAME BY FORTUNE'S DEAREST SPITE".
SONNET **89**: "SPEAK OF MY LAMENESS, AND I STRAIGHT WILL HALT".

r W.H.

But of course biographical analysis focuses much more on identifying the protagonists by hints dropped in the poems, and from discovering the mysterious dedicatee, one "Mr W.H.".

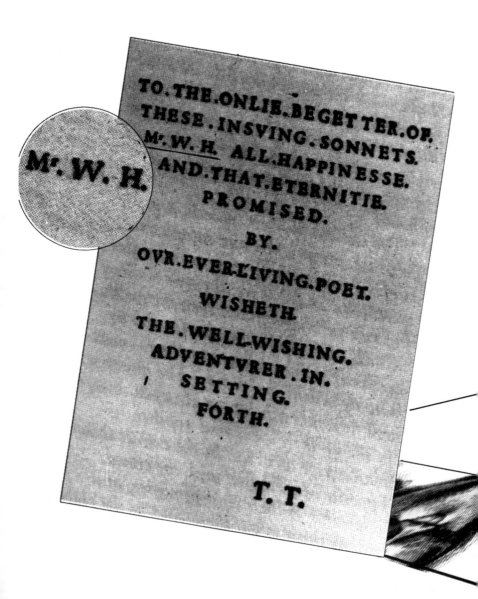

Henry Wriothesley, third Earl of Southampton, Shakespeare's patron, almost fits here (his initials are H.W. rather than W.H.). The argument runs that Shakespeare began writing sonnets to Southampton in the early 1590s, when the theatres were closed due to plague in 1592-4, and at the same time dedicated his two long poems to Southampton. Particular biographical hints about Southampton and punning on his name might fit. Shakespeare then recycled this work for **W**illiam **H**erbert, the third Earl of Pembroke, to create a composite "Young Man" figure.

Oscar Wilde's Solution

Henry Wriothesley, William Herbert, even a Mr W. Hall
("... W. H. All ..."). **Oscar Wilde** (1854-1900) wrote "The Portrait of Mr W.H." (1889), in which he presents the addressee as an effeminate young boy named Willie Hughes, an aspiring and seductive actor in Shakespeare's company who liked dressing up in girls' clothes. However, as Wilde himself disarmingly points out ...

THE ONE FLAW IN THE THEORY IS THAT IT PRESUPPOSES THE EXISTENCE OF THE PERSON WHOSE EXISTENCE IS THE SUBJECT OF DISPUTE.

Nevertheless, Wilde's lover, Lord Alfred Douglas, later became obsessed by this essay, and bizarrely discovered a real William Hewes with a possible Shakespeare connection. The suggestion of William Hewes was not in itself original, though. It was first proposed in 1766 and supported by Edmond Malone in his edition of 1780.

he Dark Lady

The Dark Lady has created the most excitement, precisely because Shakespeare does not idealize her in Sonnet 130. This sonnet has been set to music by the pop star Sting.

My mistress' eyes are nothing like the sun;
Coral is far more red than her lips' red;
If snow be white, why then her breasts are dun;
If hairs be wires, black wires grow on her head.
I have seen roses damask'd, red and white,
But no such roses see I in her cheeks,
And in some perfumes is there more delight
Than in the breath that from my mistress reeks.
I love to hear her speak, yet well I know
That music hath a far more pleasing sound;
I grant I never saw a goddess go,
My mistress when she walks treads on the ground.
　　And yet, by heaven, I think my love as rare
　　As any she belied with false compare.

ust in Action" …

Long thought to have been Mary Fitton, Pembroke's mistress, or more recently perhaps a lady-in-waiting of Elizabeth I, Aemelia Lanyer (formerly Aemelia Bassano) – she is often English, but also Italian, or a black courtesan of Clerkenwell …

The power of the Sonnets lies precisely in this desire to read Shakespeare and indeed oneself and one's theories into the lines … they are super-lubricated poetic exercises, enigmatic because Shakespeare always remains at some rhetorical distance. The truth is rather more banal.

"MR. W. H." IS LIKELY TO BE A MISPRINT FOR "MR. W. S." OR "MR. W. SH.". "BEGETTER" USUALLY MEANT THE AUTHOR RATHER THAN THE INSPIRER OF A POEM.

omantic Poets

The ability of both Shakespeare's life and verse to absorb all interpretations and still remain unperturbed intoxicated the Romantics, because it seemed to offer an essentially poetic character who had the capacity to be everything and nothing. This is, of course, much more pointed in theatre anyway – and drama and impersonation are persistent themes throughout Shakespeare's plays: "All the world's a stage", or the "poor player" who "struts and frets his hour upon the stage". This created a suggestive abyss for the Romantics.

Shakespeare is *all* and *nothing:* everyman, and hence no one in particular. It is *indeterminacy* that makes Shakespeare so powerful. He does not impose himself on his characters – they have to work out their own motives and ponder their reasons. This makes them appear to live. This is likewise the psychology of the Romantic poet.

 omantic Hamlets

But it was not just the sphinx-like Shakespeare with whom the Romantics identified. They lived through his characters too, internalized them from the page rather than in performance. Coleridge claimed that …

HAMLET WAS THE PLAY, OR RATHER *HAMLET* HIMSELF WAS THE CHARACTER, IN THE INTUITION AND EXPOSITION OF WHICH *I* FIRST MADE MY TURN FOR PHILOSOPHICAL CRITICISM ...

Coleridge lectured on Hamlet's character as …

> … all meditation, all resolution as far as words are concerned, but all hesitation and irresolution when called upon to act; so that resolving to do everything he in fact does nothing … doing nothing but resolve.

Johann Wolfgang von
Goethe
(1749-1832)

Shelley and Byron Discuss *Hamlet* ...

Percy Bysshe Shelley (1792-1822) and **Lord Byron** (1788-1824) too had a discussion on the subject, walking through the trees one evening.

BYRON — YOU SEEM VERY INEFFABLE THIS EVENING.

I HAVE BEEN READING, *HAMLET*.

NO WONDER THEN YOU ARE MELANCHOLY.

NO, 'TIS NOT SO MUCH MELANCHOLY, BUT *I* FEEL PERPLEXED, CONFUSED, AND INEXTRICABLY SELF-INVOLVED; A NIGHTMARE SENSATION OF IMPOTENCE AND VAIN ENDEAVOUR WEIGHS UPON ME, WHETHER MY OWN OR *S*HAKSPEARE'S ...

Byron goes on …

*If I had but an opinion – what can any man want more? But now I am like a nothing, a want, a privation. What **is** Hamlet? What means he? Are we, too, like him, the creatures of some incomprehensible sport, and the real universe just such another story, where all the deepest feelings, and dearest sympathies are insulted, and the understanding mocked? And yet we live on, as we read on …*

Romantic versus Modernist Hamlets

HAMLET, Prince of Denmarke.

IT IS WE WHO ARE HAMLET.

William Hazlitt

THE WHOLE OF SHAKESPEARE'S WORK IS ONE POEM; AND IT IS THE POETRY OF IT IN THIS SENSE, NOT THE POETRY OF ISOLATED LINES AND PASSAGES OR THE POETRY OF THE SINGLE FIGURES HE CREATED, THAT MATTERS MOST.

On the other hand, it was Eliot who said of *Hamlet* that it was "most certainly an artistic failure", and who heralded his form of Modernism in "The Love Song of J. Alfred Prufrock" (1915) with a direct repudiation of the Hamlet-complex …

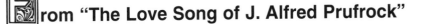

No! I am not Prince Hamlet, nor was meant to be;
Am an attendant lord, one that will do
To swell a progress, start a scene or two,
Advise the prince; no doubt, an easy tool,
Deferential, glad to be of use,
Politic, cautious, and meticulous;
Full of high sentence, but a bit obtuse;
At times, indeed, almost ridiculous –
Almost, at times, the Fool.

T.S. Eliot

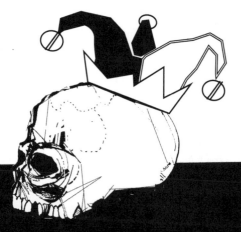

Hamlet was the ground on which Modernism
distinguished itself from Romanticism.

John Keats quoted *Hamlet* more than any other play. In a letter of August 1820 to Fanny Brawne, he writes …

> *Hamlet's heart was full of such Misery as mine is when he said to Ophelia "Go to a Nunnery, go, go!" Indeed I should like to give up the matter at one – I should like to die. I am sickened at the brute world which you are smiling with. I hate men and women more.*

He is alluding to the following speech in *Hamlet*, II.ii.303-10 …

> *What a piece of work is a man, how noble in reason, how infinite in faculties, in form and moving, how express and admirable in action, how like an angel in apprehension, how like a god! the beauty of the world; the paragon of animals; and yet to me what is this quintessence of dust? Man delights not me – nor women neither, though by your smiling you seem to say so.*

Keats's letter demonstrates the speed with which Shakespeare comes into his mind, how he thinks and feels through Shakespeare, even at his most desperate.

HAMLET HAD ALREADY BEEN QUOTED FROM THE PULPIT IN 1772. SHAKESPEARE WAS A SECULAR RELIGION.

IT WAS ALSO A POLITICAL POSITION. QUOTING HAMLET COULD BE SEEN AS A RESPONSE TO THE FRENCH REVOLUTION

Edmund Burke (1729-97), the British political conservative who wrote *Reflections on the Revolution in France* (1790), quoted *Hamlet* more than any other play by Shakespeare. More to the point, only Jesus has had more analysis than Hamlet.

Shakespeare Everywhere

In 1800, George Hardinge said, "Every thing, Sir, now-a-days has to do with Shakespeare: the difficulty is, to find out what has not to do with him". Shakespeare was already everywhere, from stage to university and intimate drawing room. In Jane Austen's *Mansfield Park* (1814), Crawford reads from Shakespeare before he and Edmund snobbishly discuss the poet.

SHAKESPEARE ONE GETS ACQUAINTED WITH WITHOUT KNOWING HOW. IT IS PART OF AN ENGLISHMAN'S CONSTITUTION.

HIS CELEBRATED PASSAGES ARE QUOTED BY EVERY BODY ... WE ALL TALK SHAKESPEARE.

Evidently, lines and passages from Shakespeare were being taken out of context.

The Biographical Pattern

But the 19th century also gave a pattern to Shakespearean ubiquity. The shape of his life was first proposed by Edward Dowden in his hugely influential primer, *Shakspere: A Critical Study of his Mind and Art* (1877), with chapters called …

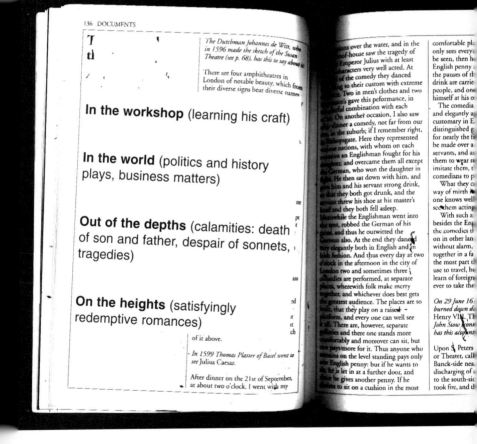

In the workshop (learning his craft)

In the world (politics and history plays, business matters)

Out of the depths (calamities: death of son and father, despair of sonnets, tragedies)

On the heights (satisfyingly redemptive romances)

The Merger of Life and Drama

The life had a clear pattern that concluded with a peaceful death. It blended Shakespeare's life with his drama, removed him from the theatre and from literary genres and traditions, and even rejected from the canon such plays as *Titus Andronicus* and *The Taming of the Shrew*.

The model was developed by the Danish critic Georg Brandes in another influential work, *William Shakespeare: A Critical Study* (three volumes, 1895-6).

Harris's biography was a series of feckless domestic tragedies: Shakespeare's flight from his jealous wife, his love for one of the Queen's Maids (the Dark Lady of the sonnets and love interest in all of the plays), the expression of his raging passions through his characters, his premature retirement in Stratford, idealizing his daughter in his final romances. Harris wondered of Hamlet (and implicitly of Shakespeare too), "Has no one made him out to be an Irishman?".

he Scholarly Project

An immense biographical project was also going on at a scholarly level. The New Shakspere Society was formed in 1874 – a close-reading project examining the metre and language of the plays in order to establish the order in which they were written.

Only in the 20th century did this interest lapse: a reflection of the modernist distrust of Shakespearean "characterization".

ejects from the Canon

Yet there was also an iconoclastic streak running through the New Shakspere Society. The first volume of its *Transactions* argued that Shakespeare did not write all of *Titus Andronicus, The Taming of the Shrew, Timon of Athens, Pericles, Henry VIII* or *The Two Noble Kinsmen.*

Rowe had rejected *Pericles*, which, despite being very popular in its own time, had not appeared in the First Folio and was added only in 1663.

Pope had doubted *Love's Labour's Lost, The Winter's Tale* and *Titus.*

Theobald was suspicious of the three parts of *Henry VI.*

Today it is admitted that not only *Timon* and *Pericles* but also even *Macbeth* have scenes not written by Shakespeare (*Timon* and *Macbeth* show the hand of **Thomas Middleton** (1580-1627), *Pericles* perhaps that of George Wilkins). *Timon* also looks unfinished, and possibly (perhaps like *Troilus and Cressida*) it was never performed during Shakespeare's lifetime – still, it remains in his collected works, and replaced *Troilus* in the First Folio, presumably for copyright reasons.

heatrical Traditions

Shakespeare has had an unbroken theatrical run since the Restoration. The 18th-century player-manager David Garrick is the prime mover here. With his rapid, naturalistic style of acting, he fixed roles like Richard III (arguably the most popular play in England in the 18th and 19th centuries), Hamlet and Macbeth.

MY PORTRAYALS WERE CANONIZED IN ACTING MANUALS ...

... AND IN PAINTINGS BY ARTISTS LIKE MYSELF, HENRY FUSELI.

Garrick's attraction was that he found expression for the quality of immensity in Shakespeare. He made the roles appear to be too large for the stage.

William Hazlitt

WE DO NOT LIKE TO SEE OUR AUTHOR'S PLAYS ACTED, AND LEAST OF ALL, *HAMLET* ... *H*AMLET HIMSELF SEEMS HARDLY CAPABLE OF BEING ACTED.

*H*IS DRAMA WILL BECOME INCAPABLE OF LIVING PERFORMANCE, AND WILL BECOME THE FRAGMENT OF A *COLOSSUS*, AN *E*GYPTIAN PYRAMID WHICH EVERYONE GAZES AT IN AMAZE-MENT AND NO ONE UNDER-STANDS.

SHAKESPEARE WAS ESCAPING FROM REPRESENTATION. *T*HE *G*ERMAN CRITIC *J*OHANN *G*OTTFRIED *H*ERDER (1744-1803) CLAIMED THAT ...

Yet these were heavily rewritten roles. **Colley Cibber** (1671-1757) had adapted *Richard III*, for example, and some of his changes were even adopted by Laurence Olivier in his own film version.

109

The Curse of *Macbeth*

There was also a darker theatrical tradition: the curse of *Macbeth*. This arose with rumours that the witches' spells were authentic magic. Early performances discovered actors really murdered on stage or in danger from collapsing scenery, or inexplicable fatalities among actors and stagehands.

Actors cross themselves or quote from *The Merchant of Venice:* "Fair thoughts and happy hours attend on you!" (III.iv.41) Or, more elaborately, turn around three times, spit, knock on the dressing-room door three times, and plead to enter.

National Theatre

The theatrical tradition of Shakespeare has been inseparable from proposals for the foundation of a national theatre ever since the early 20th-century campaign for a British National Theatre merged with a campaign for a Shakespeare memorial. In 1919, this funded the Memorial Theatre in Stratford, the first permanent repertory company.

The Old Vic, founded in the 19th century, which would become the National Theatre in 1963, was also supported by the Memorial National Theatre Committee.

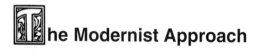he Modernist Approach

The prevalence of Shakespeare performances (and the fact that dramatists like **George Bernard Shaw** (1856-1950) sat on the Theatre Committee) emphasized the modernist qualities of Shakespeare.

This encouraged close
reading and discouraged
placing too much
emphasis on context.

THE PROTEAN SHAKESPEARE HAS AN ENDURING ATTRACTION BECAUSE HIS WORKS CAN BE CREATED ANEW WITH EACH PRODUCTION.

Sir Peter Hall

Shakespeare's indeterminacy is entirely in
tune with RSC practice – indeed, they have
often banned living playwrights from
rehearsals of their own works.

Multi-media Shakespeare

As plays were reassessed by scholars, the canon of Shakespearean adaptations grew exponentially. Reinventions made the plays live anew in other media. *Romeo and Juliet* inspired the composers Berlioz, Tchaikovsky, Prokofiev, and later Leonard Bernstein's musical *West Side Story*. *Macbeth, Othello* and *The Merry Wives of Windsor* gave Verdi the plots for his operas. The song "Who is Sylvia" from *Two Gentlemen of Verona* was arranged by Franz Schubert.

A Midsummer Night's Dream has inspired paintings, music, ballets, operas and films. This also happened at the level of character. In the 17th century, *Henry IV* was often called *Falstaff*.

OF COURSE, I HAVE MY OWN VERDI OPERA AND I'VE BECOME A TYPOLOGICAL FIGURE.

As Gary Taylor notes: "In this cultural environment Shakespeare's artistic supremacy had ceased to be debated; it was simply assumed." It has also inspired significant research into the 16th-century staging of Shakespearean plays.

nearthing the Rose Theatre

Two of Shakespeare's earliest plays were performed at Philip Henslowe's Rose Theatre, and he almost certainly acted on that stage. The foundations of the Rose were discovered during building work near Southwark Bridge at the corner of Rose Alley and Park Street, and unearthed in February 1989. The excavation revealed a polygonal building (irregular 14-sided and galleried, full-house capacity of 1,600), with a small stage 16½ feet deep, so intimate that the furthest spectator was only 50 feet away from the action. Certain scenes in *Henry VI* would have filled the space completely.

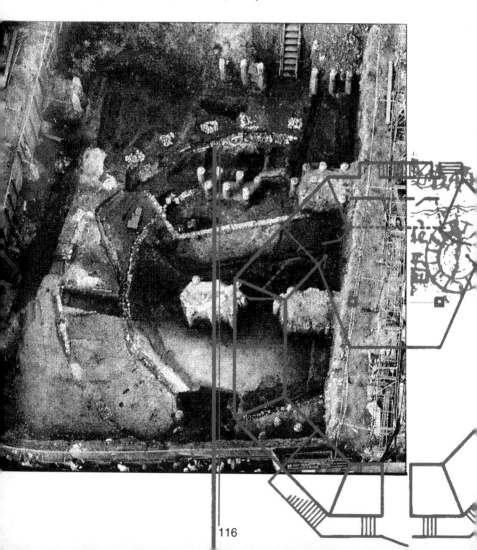

The Rose was hailed as the cradle of British theatre – the stage that Shakespeare himself trod – but it had only been uncovered because the site was about to be redeveloped. Prime Minister Margaret Thatcher offered only verbal support.

I PLACE MY FAITH IN THE FREE MARKET VALUE OF CULTURE.

BUT THE COUNTRY'S ACTORS CAME TOGETHER IN AN IMPRESSIVE SHOW OF SOLIDARITY – *IAN MCKELLEN*, *PEGGY ASHCROFT*, *JUDI DENCH*, *RALPH FIENNES* – EVEN *DUSTIN HOFFMAN* WAS THERE.

They saved the Rose in a philistine cultural environment that had been slashing subsidies to British theatre for years. Almost. Rose Court is built *over* rather than *on* the theatre, which awaits full renovation.

In the meantime, the American film and theatre impresario **Sam Wanamaker** (1919-93) built a replica of the Globe Theatre, which despite being neither on an original site nor built to exact architectural specifications, begins to occupy the imagination of modern Bardolaters. The International Shakespeare Globe Centre is built on land adjacent to the Rose, but as the Rose was concreted over, work began on the Globe.

Perhaps predictably, Adrian Noble (director of the Royal Shakespeare Company) said: "The answer is not to go back to Globe playhouses. I think that's a nonsense ... because the world has moved on."

Shakespeare in Cinema

One way the world has moved on is in
film. Shakespeare again was there at
the beginning. A scene from Herbert
Beerbohm Tree's massive production of
King John was filmed in 1899 as an early
cinematic spectacle. Shakespeare was
thenceforth capitalized by the film
industry in scores of silent films, and
afterwards when sound came.

The Spectrum of Shakespeare Films

Films of Shakespeare plays have often commented on particular political or national issues. Laurence Olivier's *Henry V*, released in 1944, was a brilliantly patriotic morale booster and a contribution to the Allied war effort.

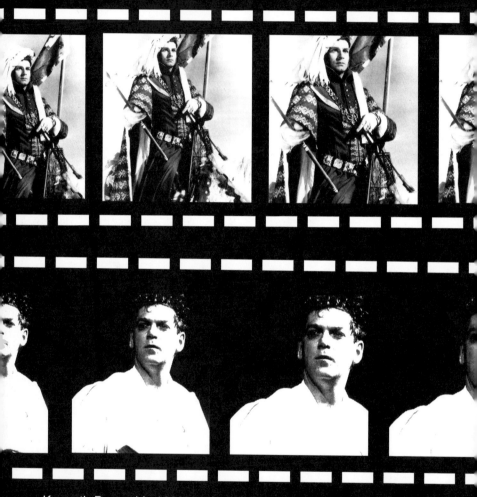

Kenneth Branagh's 1989 version of the same film turned war into a grim metaphor for grindingly claustrophobic Tory politics.

Branagh keeps returning to Shakespeare *(Much Ado About Nothing, Love's Labour's Lost),* most recently with an ambitious *Hamlet* (1996)

So does Hollywood, with Mel Gibson in *Hamlet*, Leonardo di Caprio in *Romeo and Juliet*, and even Al Pacino's musings on *Richard III*.

The experimental film-maker **Derek Jarman** (1942-94) has a long and committed engagement with Shakespeare, most flamboyantly in his idiosyncratic version of *The Tempest*, but elsewhere meditating on the sonnets.

Peter Greenaway has notoriously filmed his own *Tempest* as

inematic and TV Adaptations

Shakespearean cinema has proved as infinitely adaptable as Shakespearean theatre, perhaps more so. There have been musical adaptations, such as *The Boys from Syracuse (The Comedy of Errors)*, *Kiss Me Kate (The Taming of the Shrew)*, *West Side Story (Romeo and Juliet)* and *Return to the Forbidden Planet (The Tempest)*. Shakespeare is often quoted at length and as part of the integrity of films: in *My Own Private Idaho (Henry IV)*, *Withnail and I (Hamlet)* and *Interview with the Vampire (Othello)*. The *Complete Works* features significantly in *Star Wars IV*. This is true on the small screen as well.

The first series of the BBC TV comedy *The Black Adder* ("with additional dialogue by William Shakespeare") began with Peter Cook playing Laurence Olivier playing Richard III, and declaring …

> *Now is the summer of our sweet content*
> *Made overcast winter by these Tudor clouds.*
> *And I, that am not shaped for blackfac'd war …*
> *I that am rudely cast and want true majesty*
> *Am forced to fight to keep sweet England free.*
> *I pray to heaven we fare well.*
> *And all who fight us, go to hell!*

The first episode in particular quotes extravagantly from many of Shakespeare's plays. Once one starts looking, there are allusions and parodies everywhere: explicitly in the film *Shakespeare in Love* or implicitly as in Disney's *The Lion King* (*Hamlet*).

Shakespeare on a Global Scale

Shakespearean cinema is global. The plays translate easily into other cultures – witness *Ran*, Akira Kurosawa's Samurai film of *King Lear*. Again, it may be the lack of a dogmatic moral order that makes the material so flexible. In India too, for example, there is a rich Shakespearean tradition.

SHAKESPEARE WAS FIRST PERFORMED IN BOMBAY IN 1770, BEFORE DEVELOPING INTO A REGIONAL MUSICAL TRADITION.

IN URDU, SHAKESPEARE HAS BEEN TRANSLATED MORE THAN ANY OTHER FOREIGN AUTHOR.

HAMLET (KHUNE-NAHAQ OR UNJUST MURDER) IS STAGED AS A MUSICAL.

As in the West, the declamatory Shakespearean style of Indian acting remained well into the advent of the movies and shaped the Bollywood film industry.

ardolatry

Bardolatry (a word coined by George Bernard Shaw), or *Shakesperotics* or *Bardbiz*, is pervasive. Shakespeare is in headlines and cartoons, on cigars, in punk rock (Johnny Rotten of the Sex Pistols: "I loved *Macbeth* – a gorgeous piece of nastiness"). Shakespeare is on postage stamps, T-shirts and button badges, and even features as a hologram on some credit cards. On BBC Radio 4's long-running interview programme, *Desert Island Discs,* castaways are allowed to take ten records to their idyll, a luxury …

The World's Compulsory Author

Shakespeare has in fact received more commentary than the Bible. He is the only compulsory author in the English National Curriculum for schoolchildren. Shakespeare was also being taught extensively in American schools and colleges by the end of the 19th century.

INDEED, THE AMERICAN EDUCATION WAS BASED ON ENGLISH LITERATURE – AND THEREFORE ON SHAKESPEARE.

American tycoons began assembling collections of Shakespeare folios and quartos, which led eventually to the foundation of great libraries like the Pierpont Morgan (New York) and the Folger Shakespeare Library (on Capitol Hill in Washington DC). Elsewhere, there is a Globe Theatre in Tokyo. Shakespeare permeates both popular culture and academic discourse.

The Englishness of Shakespeare?

Is this cosmopolitan Shakespeare – available worldwide – still a defining model of Englishness? Or is this an example of English cultural imperialism? The problem of resorting to Shakespeare for definitions of Englishness is that he is just as interested in *Britishness*, albeit at a time when "Britain" did not exactly mean the same thing as it does today. For example, in *Henry V* (III.iii.122-4), the Irish officer Macmorris wonders …

Is there a German Shakespeare?

Shakespeare has been enlisted as a characteristically Gothic writer, free from classical restraint and intimately connected with the land. This is why he was so rapidly absorbed into Teutonic culture by Goethe and the German Romanticists at the end of the 18th century.

The first play of his that I read made me his for life … I stood like one born blind, on whom a miraculous hand bestows sight in a moment. I saw, I felt, in the most vivid manner, that my existence was infinitely expanded.

So deep was the German identification with Shakespeare that he was used in anti-British propaganda during the First World War.

nd Now a European Shakespeare?

This national partisanship has changed since the Second World War. The post-war suspicion of "leader characters" – men who can bend a society, even a nation, to their will – has been mediated by attending to other equally charismatic but less dictatorial and more communal figures. So too, the biographical conception of Shakespeare has shifted to the cosmopolitan.

The Criticism of Close Reading

Criticism of Shakespeare in the first half of the 20th century focused on "close reading" rather than character. The whole critical practice of close reading was virtually a side-effect of analysing individual sonnets. The English poet and writer Robert Graves turned Shakespeare into a Modernist. The influential critic William Empson used the Sonnets to illustrate his famous theory of "seven types of ambiguity". The Russian pioneer of semiotics Roman Jakobson turned Shakespeare into a semiotician.

William Empson

Roman Jakobson

Robert Graves

ALL ONE NEEDED WAS A "COMMUNAL" TEXT.

This rarefied aesthetic activity was already being challenged by Shakespearean directors like the German dramatist **Bertolt Brecht** (1898-1956). Brecht was a Marxist whose plays and adaptations were actively anti-capitalist and anti-fascist.

MY FAVOURITE TECHNIQUE WAS TO "ALIENATE" AUDIENCES FROM THE CHARACTERS AND ACTION ONSTAGE TO PREVENT EASY IDENTIFICATION AND SYMPATHY.

Jan Kott (b. 1914), a professor of literature in Warsaw, adapted Brecht's ideas in his influential book *Shakespeare Our Contemporary* (1961). Kott reads Shakespeare in order to memorialize the tyrannies of Hitler and Stalin, rather than lose sight of them in Elizabethan researches or self-indulgent close reading. Shakespeare's universal genius becomes apparent in the immediate solutions he could offer in current political affairs. If Shakespeare is immortal, Kott reasons, then he must be as relevant today as he was in the 16th century.

Kott's deliberate humanitarian policy of reading topical problems into Shakespeare inspired a generation of theatrical productions and prompted numerous critical revaluations. Postmodern theoreticians tend instead to do the opposite and situate the works of Shakespeare in political, economic, ideological, gendered and sexed, or colonial and post-colonial contexts, either to reveal their suppressed radical subversions, or to expose their unsound presumptions.

THE READER IS THEREFORE READING DOUBLE ...

... BOTH ENGAGED WITHIN THE PLAY, BUT AT THE SAME TIME OUTSIDE IT, JUDGING THE PROTAGONISTS BY OUR OWN CONTEMPORARY STANDARDS.

THIS MAY BE EXCITINGLY ICONOCLASTIC, BUT IT IS IDÉE FIXE CRITICISM.

Denis Donoghue has suggested that "literary critics of our time are lunatics of one idea, and ... are celebrated in the degree of the ferocity with which they enforce it".

THEY PRIZE TEXTS THAT CONFIRM THEIR PRECONCEPTIONS ...

BUT THEY NEVER SEEM TO WONDER WHY THEY ARE READING ME IN THE FIRST PLACE.

Ironically, even this reductive attention to Shakespeare tends to universalize him further.

⧉outhpiece of the Conservative Establishment

Shakespeare is currently under attack for being a poodle of the Establishment – a pejorative use of the title "National Poet". The argument runs that, historically, Shakespeare has been adapted to conservatism.

His position in schools or at large in culture is a clear example of the bourgeoisie's attempt to reproduce their class ideology. This was made most explicit by Margaret Thatcher's Secretary of State for Education, Kenneth Baker.

Shakespeare is a fundamental principle in English education, let alone in many English courses over the globe. Merely brief attempts to gain familiarity with certain plays will determine how those works will be taught and read, and certain assumptions about how to read and write will be communicated – in particular those which treat him outside history, rather than as part of historical process. And anyway, Shakespeare is the archetypal Dead White European Male writer.

The Political Misuse of Shakespeare

Shakespeare can be used to support conservatism. Ulysses' speech in defence of order (*Troilus and Cressida*, I.iii.109-10) has often been quoted by Tory politicians as if Shakespeare were endorsing it.

*T*AKE BUT DEGREE AWAY, UNTUNE THAT STRING, AND HARK WHAT DISCORD FOLLOWS.

*B*UT THAT SPEECH IS IN THE MOUTH OF A CHARACTER WHO IS BY TURNS CALCULATING, SARDONIC AND TRIFLING.

Shakespeare can also be used to defend forces of repression. In Communist Eastern Europe, Shakespeare was taught as an instrument of Marxist dogma.

HE IS FREQUENTLY ALLUDED TO IN *MARX'S* WRITING ...

MARX QUOTES FROM *TIMON OF ATHENS* AND CONCLUDES ...

SHAKESPEARE PORTRAYS THE ESSENCE OF MONEY EXCELLENTLY.

Shakespeare can also be used – and has been used – by other social groups and indeed in radical politics – most obviously in his time by Essex's rebels sponsoring a performance of *Richard II* to justify their revolt against Elizabeth I.

ew Historicism

The concept "New Historicism" was coined by Stephen Greenblatt in 1982. It aims to explain how a culture's various forms of expression (such as literature, religion, ritual) make up a society and endorse its values at specific historical times. New Historicism denies that these forms of expression have anything more than "anthropological" significance, but should be interpreted in the contexts of politics and institutional power, class and gender conditions, and the economic forces of production and imperialism.

THE POINT IS TO REVEAL HOW LITERATURE EITHER CONSPIRES WITH THE FORCES OF OPPRESSION OR SUBVERTS THEM.

NEW HISTORICISM IS HIGHLY INTERDISCIPLINARY CRITICISM ...

It juxtaposes literature with other, often surprising, texts – scientific, medical, legal, theological, and so forth – and turns Shakespeare into an interactive jigsaw piece in Elizabethan and Jacobean culture.

The effect is to erode Shakespeare's exceptional status by drawing historical analogies and incorporating him into his society. An example is the "appropriation" of Shakespeare's theatrical troupe by James I, which made them the "King's Men".

Shakespeare's subsequent plays are then assumed to explore these regal "ideologies". The most interesting question here perhaps is whether Shakespeare is always able to *reveal the assumptions* implicit in his society.

ultural Materialism

Cultural Materialism is founded on Marxist assumptions and therefore considers criticism to be a form of political resistance, both in condemning the past and "challenging" the present. It is not dissimilar to New Historicism and is influenced by the same theorists (Michel Foucault, Louis Althusser, Raymond Williams and Clifford Geertz), but focused more in the present than in the past. It is defined by two of its exponents as "a combination of historical context, theoretical method, political commitment and textual analysis".

> *TEXTS* ARE EXAMINED AS PLACES WHERE IDEOLOGICAL POWER AND ILLUSION IS CONSOLIDATED, SUBVERTED OR CONTAINED.

> *THIS* IS EVIDENT IN THE HUNT FOR "MARGINALIZED VOICES" – MINORITY GROUPS CONSIDERED SUBVERSIVE AT THE TIME WHO ARE LIKELY TO HAVE BEEN EXCLUDED FROM THE HISTORICAL RECORD.

Again, all this is designed to dismantle the universality of Shakespeare. Yet Cultural Materialism considers itself to be a universal system. If not as monumental as Marxism, it is at least as comprehensive as Foucault's theories, and preoccupied with the same questions of identity and power relations.

Cultural Materialism has literally very little to do with criticism, except by enlisting it in political battles over the current teaching of literature. Everything is either reduced to politics or ignored. For Cultural Materialists, literature is either an emancipation from social oppression or it is collusive with power.

Rulers too had few qualms about stating precisely their policies of control. In his *Book of Sports* (1618), James I declared that energetic games and festivals were one way of defusing popular unrest. Not much mystification there, then.

The Late Capitalist Show

Cultural Materialism's main preoccupation is with the present rather than the past. For instance, the contemporary Marxist critic Terry Eagleton asserts...

Some materialist critics have taken their obsession with commodities and the market to even greater lengths …

The complexity of the plays might be described not as an artistic achievement but rather as a shrewd strategy to curry favour with as many sectors as possible within a complex multi-cultural market. This would suggest that a Shakespearean work is in effect an industrial rather than an individual product and that its specific form of appearance is in some fundamental way motivated and sanctioned by an ethos of business success. Shakespeare would then be seen as something more like a modern corporate logo or trademark rather than a specific name of an exceptional individual or creative genius.

 # ost-Colonial Criticism

The Tempest has been a favourite text of Post-Colonial critics, who take it as an opportunity to research British colonial operations from Ireland to outpost Third World countries. But *The Tempest* can also be rewritten as penetrating social satire, as Aldous Huxley did in his vision of a future dystopia, *Brave New World*.

"*O* BRAVE NEW WORLD / *T*HAT HAS SUCH PEOPLE IN'T", SAYS *M*IRANDA IN THE LAST SCENE OF THE PLAY – WHICH LOOKS FORWARD TO A WORLD OF GENETIC CLONES.

The text is pregnant with possibility, especially in the figures of Caliban and Sycorax. Some writers have taken these figures and woven new stories about them.

MUCH AS JEAN RHYS DID WHEN SHE WROTE THE UNTOLD STORY OF BERTHA MASON IN WIDE SARGASSO SEA, WHO APPEARS AS THE MAD WOMAN IN MY JANE EYRE (1847).

Charlotte Brontë

Caribbean paradise

Shakespeare can be vilified, or co-opted, or his writing can provide the grounds for a rethinking of Jacobean imperialism. On the other hand, *The Tempest* can also be read as an experimental comedy and a final riposte to the long-dead Marlowe's satanic *Doctor Faustus*.

Shakespeare's Views on Race?

But Post-Colonial rereadings of Shakespeare did not start with New Historicist revelations that *The Tempest* is a "discourse of imperialism". The critique has a rich background among Caribbean writers like George Lamming, Edward Kamau Brathwaite and Aimé Césaire. Shakespeare is in any case very concerned with racial difference. His first black character is Aaron in *Titus Andronicus* (Shakespeare may have played the role himself), who glories in his colour (IV.ii.97-103) …

What, what, ye sanguine, shallow-hearted boys!
Ye white-lim'd walls! ye alehouse painted signs!
Coal-black is better than another hue,
In that it scorns to bear another hue;
For all the water in the ocean
Can never turn the swan's black legs to white,
Although she lave them hourly in the flood.

Despite this, some critics have complained that white is assumed as a standard of beauty and sexual attraction in Shakespeare, forgetting too that his most alluring character is of course Cleopatra.

Curiously neglected by recent commentators, from the insistence on her "dun" complexion she should really be called the "Black Woman" rather than the Dark Lady. It has been argued that she may have been based on a black courtesan called Lucy Negro (Sonnets 127-52).

Shylock in *The Merchant of Venice* does however present the problem of anti-Semitism. Although he is not a racist type but a complex character in himself, the play is difficult to deal with after the Holocaust.

Feminist Criticism

New Historicism and Cultural Materialism have been criticized for under-representing Feminist contributions. In fact, a Feminist tradition in Shakespeare criticism goes back at least to 1736 when the Shakespeare Ladies Club lobbied the London theatres at Drury Lane and Covent Garden for more revivals of Shakespearean plays.

Early female critics were influential: Charlotte Lennox (*Shakespeare Illustrated,* 1753); Eliza Haywood (*The Female Spectator,* 1755); Elizabeth Montagu (*An Essay on the Genius of Shakespeare*, 1769); and Elizabeth Griffith (*The Morality of Shakespeare's Drama Illustrated*, 1775). They culminated in the shape of Henrietta Maria Bowdler, who in 1807 published *The Family Shakespeare.*

The Family Shakespeare was an edition of twenty plays ...

It is, incidentally, here that concern is first aired regarding the immorality of *Measure for Measure* (a play intimately driven by sexual urges). By the end of the 19th century it had become a "problem play", a prime example of Victorian sexual mores. (Critics have also puzzled over whether Hamlet actually slept with Ophelia – to which an old actor-manager once replied, "In our company – always!")

Twentieth-Century Feminist Criticism

Shakespeare was used by **Virginia Woolf** (1882-1941) in her seminal essay, *A Room of One's Own* (1929).

Woolf's essay is elegant and effective. There is, however, a tendency for late 20th-century Feminist criticism and productions to emphasize the victimization and exploitation of women in plays.

Accounts of *The Taming of the Shrew*, for example, ignore the complicit irony of Kate. Indeed, it is in this play that Shakespearean ambiguity or indeterminacy first appears.

AS IF *I* HADN'T QUITE MADE UP MY OWN MIND ABOUT MY CHARACTERS.

AND THEN HE CHARACTERISTICALLY COMPLICATES THE QUESTIONS BY HALF-FRAMING THE PIECE AS A PLAY OR A DREAM.

John Fletcher tried to answer some of the questions in his continuation called *The Woman's Prize, or the Tamer Tamed* (1604), in which Petruchio's second wife locks him out on their wedding night and hence tames *him* …

# The Gender Question

Current Feminist approaches tend to examine patriarchal power and gender production in Shakespeare. Certainly his later works are characterized by problems with women, protectiveness against female sexuality, and an obsession with the father-daughter relationship.

KING LEAR CAN BE SEEN AS A REPRESENTATION OF PATRIARCHAL MISOGYNY AND A LESSON IN FAMILY DUTY ...

ONLY THOSE WHO COLLUDE IN MISOGYNY CAN ENDORSE THE ENDING.

Yet such approaches risk being reductive and simplistic, ignoring dramatic causality (the necessities of plot) and character (who says what to whom, and where and when in the play they say it). They also risk advocating the very same binary oppositions of gender that they declare to be challenging.

Feminist approaches have in turn created a subset of body criticism, dissecting the Renaissance idea of the body through investigations of, for example, medical texts, and therefore conjuring more "contexts" for Shakespeare plays. This has also created great excitement about sexual identities on the Shakespearean stage.

PARTICULARLY IF WE BEAR IN MIND THAT FEMALE CHARACTERS WERE PLAYED BY CROSS-DRESSED BOYS ...

ALTHOUGH FAR TOO MUCH HAS BEEN MADE OF "TRANSVESTISM" AND HOMOEROTICISM. IT WAS NOT ONLY A THEATRICAL CONVENTION BUT A *LEGAL* REQUIREMENT.

And if we recall how often Shakespeare's heroines disguise themselves anyway, the boys playing them could be comfortably attired as men for a considerable part of their "female" role. And it is the sort of thing one barely notices reading the play, away from the stage. On the other hand, it is worth considering how the portrayal of *female* characters by female actors, or a *black* actor playing Aaron or Othello, changes that role onstage.

ueer Theory

It was suggested as early as 1824 that Shakespeare may have been homosexual, but Queer Theory (Gay criticism) finds little to say about the plays …

Although the Sonnets are really "pre-homosexual", their critical heritage is of great interest in the genesis of 20th-century homosexual politics.

Psychoanalytic Criticism

Psychoanalytic readings of Shakespeare take their cue from **Sigmund Freud** (1856-1939) and later from the "French Freud", **Jacques Lacan** (1901-81). Freud fancied himself a critic of *Hamlet*, in which he predictably saw a dramatization of the Oedipus Complex.

Freud psychoanalysed Hamlet in *The Interpretation of Dreams* (1900), and claimed to have finally solved its theme: "I have translated into conscious terms what was bound to remain unconscious in Hamlet's mind."

Hamlet is a good psychoanalytic patient who admits to the shrink …

Bearing in mind the extent to which Shakespeare inspired (or wrote) Freud and his theories, it is not surprising that the American Shakespeare scholar Harold Bloom finds Shakespeare to be the more sensitive instrument of psychology.

INCREASINGLY IT SEEMS TO ME THAT LITERATURE, AND PARTICULARLY SHAKESPEARE, WHO IS LITERATURE, IS A MUCH MORE COMPREHENSIVE MODE OF COGNITION THAN PSYCHOANALYSIS CAN BE.

IN ANY CASE, THERE IS AN IRONY IN THE FREUDIAN ANALYSIS OF SHAKESPEARE ...

FREUD BEGAN AS A "GROUPIST", BELIEVING THAT SHAKESPEARE WAS A COLLABORATION OF SEVERAL DIFFERENT PLAYWRIGHTS.

THEN I THOUGHT HE WAS A FRENCHMAN CALLED JACQUES PIERRE, BEFORE I DECIDED THAT EDWARD DE VERE, EARL OF OXFORD, WROTE IT ALL.

uthorship Controversy

The authorship controversy persists because despite some two or three dozen official and legal documents that mention Shakespeare, and possibly threescore contemporary allusions, we still need to know more about his personal life. His plays show familiarity with the law, with the court, and with classical learning: he must have been highly educated.

hakespeare Gets his Bacon

Nobody thought that Shakespeare wasn't the author of his own plays until the end of the 18th century, and the idea only became popular more than *two centuries* after his death. This suggests that there was a different idea of Shakespeare prevalent – and also a different idea of authorship current – during those 200 years. Baconianism, the theory that **Francis Bacon** (1561-1626) wrote Shakespeare, is essentially promulgated in *The Story of the Learned Pig* (1786).

THIS IS A TALE OF REINCARNATION IN WHICH "*PIMPING BILLY*" – CURRENTLY IN THE SHAPE OF A PERFORMING PIG – CLAIMS AUTHORSHIP OF A TROTTERFUL OF *SHAKESPEARE'S* PLAYS (INCLUDING, OF COURSE, *HAM-LET*).

THIS NONSENSE HAD BEEN RATHER MORE SERIOUSLY PROPOSED BY REVD *JAMES WILMOT* IN *1785* ...

SHAKESPEARE – AT BEST A COUNTRY CLOWN – LACKED THE NECESSARY EDUCATION TO COMPOSE THE PLAYS. *HENCE* THEY WERE THE WORK OF *FRANCIS BACON*.

But Wilmot burnt his papers in shame before he died, and his theory only came to light a century and a half later.

ther Bacon Partisans

Baconianism was most energetically (if insanely) promoted in the 19th century by an American autodidact, Delia Bacon. Staying with the influential Victorian critic **Thomas Carlyle** (1795-1881), she declared …

MUCH AS *I* RESPECT YOU, *MR CARLYLE*, *I* MUST TELL YOU THAT YOU DO NOT KNOW WHAT IS REALLY IN THE *PLAYS* IF YOU BELIEVE THAT THAT *BOOBY* WROTE THEM.

I SIMPLY LAUGHED MY HEAD OFF …

But she had her supporters, and even spent an evening in Holy Trinity Church, Stratford …

Ex-Prime Minister and bellicose Foreign Secretary Lord Palmerston became a convert to Baconianism via the work of William Henry Smith.

161

ecoding Shakespeare

Ignatius Donnelly, "prince of crackpots", was another driven Baconian who, like many of his fellow "Anti-Stratfordians", had trained as a lawyer and consequently believed that "Shakespeare" must have done so as well.

> *I* ASSIGN NOT ONLY THE WORKS OF **S**HAKESPEARE TO **B**ACON, BUT ALSO THE **S**HAKESPEARE APOCRYPHA, *M*ONTAIGNE'*S* *E*SSAYS, *B*URTON'S *A*NATOMY OF *M*ELANCHOLY, SOME OF *G*EORGE *P*EELE'S WORKS, AND ALL OF *C*HRISTOPHER *M*ARLOWE ...

Donnelly's masterpiece was *The Great Cryptogram*, in which he decoded Shakespeare according to a cipher he had discovered in a children's magazine.

Cryptograms, Ciphers and Acrostics

Much Baconian "research" involved (and still involves) identifying fiendish ciphers in Shakespeare's texts – in the First Folio, for example – or in making anagrams of particular words. It is also a tactic of the Anti-Stratfordians to treat the Sonnets as a cryptic autobiography, despite the overwhelming historical evidence that Elizabethans did not write such things. In at least one case, the Baconian cryptoanalyst Orville Owen received instructions on the cipher used from Bacon's obliging ghost.

In 1610, the King James translation of the Bible was being finalized. It has been proposed that Shakespeare, dramatist of the King's Men, was consulted – and even wrote part of it. In Psalm 46, "God is our refuge and strength, a very present help in trouble", the 46th word from the beginning is *shake*, and the 46th from the end is *spear*. In 1610, Shakespeare was 46 years old …

The librettist of the classic operettas, **W.S.Gilbert** (1836-1911), perhaps offered the best solution.

DO YOU KNOW HOW THEY ARE GOING TO DECIDE THE SHAKESPEARE-BACON DISPUTE? THEY ARE GOING TO DIG UP SHAKESPEARE AND DIG UP BACON ...

THEY ARE GOING TO SET THEIR COFFINS SIDE-BY-SIDE, AND THEY ARE GOING TO GET HERBERT BEERBOHM TREE TO RECITE HAMLET TO THEM.

AND THE ONE WHO TURNS IN HIS COFFIN WILL BE THE AUTHOR OF THE PLAY.

There have been others proposed as the author of Shakespeare's plays. It was suggested in 1824 that Shakespeare began his acting career under the name "Christopher Marlowe", and Marlowe was later seriously proposed as the author of the plays – despite the fact that his death in 1593 was heavily documented. Other dramatic contemporaries like Peele and Chapman have been candidates, but there are less predictable ones.

The Oxford Controversy – and Looney Tunes

But the most enduring counterclaim to Bacon has been Edward de Vere, **Earl of Oxford** (1550-1604) – a theory first advanced by one J. Thomas Looney *(sic!)* and supported by Freud. Not simply courtly, worldly and educated like Bacon, Oxford was an *aristocrat*, and Looney emphasized the aristocracy inherent in Shakespeare. He won considerable support.

THE OXFORDIAN THEORIES ARE CERTAINLY AS LAUGHABLE AS THE BACONIAN THEORIES, BUT WORSE, THEY ARE SNOBBISH AS WELL.

THERE HAVE EVEN BEEN SHOW TRIALS IN WHICH THE STRATFORD MAN IS SUED BY OXFORD ...

Although in at least one case this did serve to raise money for the Globe Theatre project. Anyway, Oxford died in 1604 and so the claim cannot be seriously sustained, because several plays make allusions to contemporary events occurring *after* that date.

Although it has to be said that the majority of these ridiculous authorship claims are made by amateur American "scholars", it does appeal to the English sense of class superiority as well. Sir Charles Spencer Chaplin judged that …

nd So, in Conclusion

Harold Bloom, who charmingly calls himself "Bloom Brontosaurus Bardolater", argues that Shakespeare created characters that develop rather than unfold, often by overhearing themselves talking. In doing so, Shakespeare created more than modes of expression, patterns of words and language, or typologies – he invented the *modern human character*. Bloom sees archetypally human characters in the indeterminate vigour of Rosalind, Falstaff, Hamlet, Iago, Lear and Cleopatra.

THE PLAYS REMAIN THE OUTWARD LIMIT OF HUMAN ACHIEVEMENT: AESTHETICALLY, COGNITIVELY, IN CERTAIN WAYS MORALLY, EVEN SPIRITUALLY. THEY ABIDE BEYOND THE END OF THE MIND'S REACH; WE CANNOT CATCH UP TO THEM.

Bloom's response is to Cultural Materialists like Terence Hawkes, who argues that there is no essential meaning to Shakespeare's texts (or, it seems, to anything), just complexes of signs: "[T]he plays have the same function as, and work like, the words of which they are made ... Shakespeare doesn't mean: *we* mean *by* Shakespeare."

In a sense these two critics agree, except that for Bloom, this situation suffices because it challenges and stretches and liberates the critical imagination. It creates readers who are alive and alert.

The contemporary critic Frank Kermode is such a reader. He reads Shakespeare closely, as poetry, but is also alive to the poetry of stagecraft. The great Russian novelist Leo Tolstoy noticed one effect that Kermode finds so uncanny in Shakespeare's lines:

> SHAKESPEARE'S CHARACTERS ... IN MOMENTS OF GREAT AGITATION, REPEAT A QUESTION SEVERAL TIMES, OR SEVERAL TIMES DEMAND THE REPETITION OF A WORD WHICH HAS PARTICULARLY STRUCK THEM, AS DO OTHELLO, MACDUFF, CLEOPATRA, AND OTHERS.

This repetition and doubling does what Ben Jonson admired in Shakespeare's verse four centuries ago – the lively turning of familiar material: "turne the same, And himselfe with it", and us with it too – turning us into human beings …

169

The Editing of Shakespeare's Texts

The most important recent developments in Shakespeare studies have been in textual criticism and new editions. There are dozens of editions currently available, for no one edition is wholly adequate. In varying degrees, they present themselves as both accessible modern versions and historical documents, as both performance scripts and reading texts.

These editorial problems recently came to a head with the convincing demonstration that the Quarto and Folio texts of *King Lear* were effectively different plays whose conflation into a single version was a hangover from 18th-century editorial practice that assumed they shared a single source. To much controversy, Stanley Wells and Gary Taylor's edition of the *Complete Works* published by the Clarendon Press, Oxford in 1986 printed the two versions of *Lear* separately (one a "History", the other a "Tragedy"). This followed a debate described by Gary Taylor and Michael Warren in *The Division of the Kingdoms* (1983) and summarized by Gary Taylor in *Reinventing Shakespeare* (1990).

The History of King Lear is derived from a Quarto edition of 1608; *The Tragedy of King Lear* from the Folio text (1623). Shakespeare appears to have been in the habit of tinkering with his work, as the different texts of *Othello*, for example, show. But with *Lear*, the argument is that the *Tragedy* is not simply a light revision of the earlier *History*, but a substantial rewrite: in effect, it is a new play. In addition to many minor revisions, the *Tragedy* cuts the mock trial, develops the characterization and charisma of Goneril, reduces the role of Albany and rewrites much of Kent's part. The overall effect is to excise moral commentary and darken the play, and to strengthen the roles of Cordelia and Edgar. The *Tragedy*, dated to 1609-10, can be grouped with late plays like *Cymbeline*.

The mistake of editors has been to conflate the two, and invent a hybrid third version that Shakespeare never composed and that the King's Men never acted, but which has been read and acted regularly in the past century or so. It is worth remembering that when John Keats inscribed his sonnet "On sitting down to read King Lear once again" into his edition of Shakespeare, he was reading a different *Lear* to the version we read today. He possessed a facsimile of the Folio edition, and would therefore have read the text of the *Tragedy*, which until recently was rejected as inadequate and incomplete.

So, the case of the two *Lears* raises important editorial questions. Keats was specifically reading and re-reading the *Tragedy*. From the 1590s onwards, the sale of Quartos had ensured a reading audience for Shakespeare, alongside the performances. With the publication of the First Folio – and then the closing of the theatres under Cromwell – Shakespeare's survival was as much due to *being read* as it had been to *being played*. By the 18th century, only heavily rewritten adaptations were performed at the theatre, and editions were marketed to readers who would read in private.

Samuel Johnson (on *Lear* again): "*I was many years ago so shocked by Cordelia's death, that I know not whether I ever endured to read again the last scenes of the play till I undertook to revise them as an editor.*"

There may be many Shakespeares, but from the scholarly debates, two identifiable traditions emerge: one in which his work is *played* before an audience, and one in which it is silently *read*. The Wells and Taylor edition, with its two *Lears*, is a brilliant work of theatre scholarship. It endeavours to print the most "theatrical" version of each play – in other words, the version closest to that which would have been played in Shakespeare's time. But in doing so, it erases generations of critical finessing which has arrived at texts that might be the product of dozens of editors and critics, effectively collaborating over generations. This minute and protracted attention has helped to create the language of literary expression, and even, according to some critics, enabled the human to fully realize itself. So we need two editions: a performance text and a reading text. The current Oxford edition is perhaps the definitive example of a performance text – the most reliable account of how Shakespeare was probably performed in his lifetime. For a reading text cultivated by critics, the individual Arden plays (currently in their third edition) remain the most comprehensive, and the Riverside the most convenient. All direct quotations in my text are taken from *The Riverside Shakespeare*, ed. G. Blakemore Evans, Harry Levin, Herschel Baker, Anne Barton, Frank Kermode, Hallett Smith, Marie Edel and Charles H. Shattuck (Boston: Houghton Mifflin, 1974). I have also consulted *William Shakespeare: The Complete Works*, ed. Stanley Wells, Gary Taylor, John Jowett and William Montgomery (Oxford: Clarendon Press, 1988).

Chronology of Shakespeare's Plays and Poems

Titles and suggested dates are based on Wells and Taylor's *Oxford Shakespeare*.

Hamlet [the "*Ur-Hamlet*"; lost work] (late 1580s/early 1590s)
The Two Gentlemen of Verona (late 1580s/early 1590s)
The Taming of the Shrew (late 1580s/early 1590s)
The First Part of the Contention of the Two Famous Houses of York and Lancaster [*Henry VI, Part 2*] (early 1590s)
The True Tragedy of Richard Duke of York and the Good King Henry the Sixth [*Henry VI, Part 3*] (before 1592)
The First Part of Henry the Sixth [*Henry VI, Part 1*] (c. 1592)
The Tragedy of King Richard the Third (c. 1592-3)
Venus and Adonis (1592-3)
The Most Lamentable Roman Tragedy of Titus Andronicus (c. 1593)
The Rape of Lucrece (c. 1593)
The Comedy of Errors (c. 1594)
Love's Labour's Lost (c. 1594)
Love's Labour's Won [lost work] (before 1598)
Sir Thomas More [partly attributed to Shakespeare] (c. 1594-5)
The Most Excellent and Lamentable Tragedy of Romeo and Juliet (c. 1594-5)
A Midsummer Night's Dream (c. 1594-5)
The Tragedy of King Richard the Second (c. 1595)
The Life and Death of King John (c. 1595-6)
The Comical History of the Merchant of Venice, or Otherwise Called the Jew of Venice (c. 1596-7)
The History of Henry the Fourth [*Henry IV, Part 1*] (c. 1596-7)
The Merry Wives of Windsor (1597)
The Second Part of Henry the Fourth (c. 1597-8)
Much Ado About Nothing (c. 1598-9)
The Life of Henry the Fifth (1599)
The Tragedy of Julius Caesar (1599)
As You Like It (c. 1599-1600)
The Tragedy of Hamlet, Prince of Denmark (c. 1600-1)
"The Phoenix and the Turtle" (1601)
Twelfth Night, or What You Will (c. 1601-2)
Troilus and Cressida (c. 1601-2)
The Sonnets and "A Lover's Complaint" (pub. 1599-1609)
All's Well That Ends Well (1602-3)
Measure for Measure (c. 1604)

The Tragedy of Othello, the Moor of Venice (c. 1603-4)
The Life of Timon of Athens (? 1604)
The History of King Lear (c. 1605)
The Tragedy of Macbeth (c. 1606)
The Tragedy of Antony and Cleopatra (c. 1606)
Pericles, Prince of Tyre (c. 1607-8)
The Tragedy of Coriolanus (c. 1607-8)
The Winter's Tale (c. 1609-10)
The Tragedy of King Lear (c. 1609-10)
Cymbeline, King of Britain (c. 1610-11)
The Tempest (1611)
Cardenio [lost work] (c. 1612-13)
All Is True [*Henry VIII*] (c. 1612-13)
The Two Noble Kinsmen (c. 1612-13)

Selected Bibliography

Jonathan Bate, *The Genius of Shakespeare* (London: Picador, 1997).
Jonathan Bate, *The Romantics on Shakespeare* (Harmondsworth: Penguin, 1992).
Harold Bloom, *Shakespeare: The Invention of the Human* (London: Fourth Estate, 1999).
Michael Bristol, *Big-Time Shakespeare* (London and New York: Routledge, 1996).
E.K. Chambers, *William Shakespeare: A Study of Facts and Problems*, 2 vols (Oxford: Clarendon Press, 1930).
Kate Chedgzoy, *Shakespeare's Queer Children: Sexual Politics and Contemporary Culture* (Manchester and New York: Manchester University Press, 1995).
Jonathan Dollimore and Alan Sinfield (eds), *Political Shakespeare: Essays in Cultural Materialism* (Manchester and New York: Manchester University Press, 1994).
John Drakakis (ed.), *Alternative Shakespeares* (London and New York: Routledge, 1985).
Terry Eagleton, *William Shakespeare* (Oxford: Blackwell, 1986).
John Elsom, *Is Shakespeare Still Our Contemporary?* (London and New York: Routledge, 1989).
William Empson, *Essays on Shakespeare*, ed. David Pirie (Cambridge: Cambridge University Press, 1986).
Marjorie Garber, *Shakespeare's Ghost Writers: Literature as Uncanny Causality* (New York and London: Methuen, 1987).
Stephen Greenblatt, *Shakespearean Negotiations: The Circulation of Social Energy* (Berkeley: University of California Press, 1988).

Terence Hawkes (ed.), *Alternative Shakespeares Volume 2* (London and New York: Routledge, 1996).

Terence Hawkes, *Meaning by Shakespeare* (London and New York: Routledge, 1992).

Terence Hawkes, *That Shakespeherian Rag: Essays on a Critical Process* (London and New York: Routledge, 1986).

Graham Holderness (ed.), *The Shakespeare Myth* (Manchester: Manchester University Press, 1988).

Park Honan, *Shakespeare: A Life* (Oxford: Oxford University Press, 1998).

John Joughin (ed.), *Shakespeare and National Culture* (Manchester and New York: Manchester University Press, 1997).

Jan Kott, *Shakespeare Our Contemporary*, tr. Boleslaw Taborski (London: Methuen, 1965).

Carol Lenz, Ruth Swift, Gayle Green and Carol Thomas Neely (eds), *The Woman's Part: Feminist Criticism of Shakespeare* (Urbana: University of Illinois Press, 1980).

Lawrence Levine, *Highbrow/Lowbrow: The Emergence of Cultural Hierarchy in America* (Cambridge, MA: Harvard University Press, 1990).

Charles and Michelle Martindale, *Shakespeare and the Uses of Antiquity* (London and New York, 1994).

Samuel Schoenbaum, *Shakespeare's Lives* (Oxford: Clarendon Press, 1991).

Gary Taylor, *Reinventing Shakespeare: A Cultural History from the Restoration to the Present* (London: Hogarth Press, 1990).

Gary Taylor and Michael Warren (eds), *The Division of the Kingdoms: Shakespeare's Two Versions of* King Lear (Oxford: Clarendon Press, 1983).

Brian Vickers, *Shakespeare: The Critical Heritage*, 6 vols (London, Henley, and Boston: Routledge & Kegan Paul, 1974-81).

Brian Vickers, *Appropriating Shakespeare: Contemporary Critical Quarrels* (New Haven and London: Yale University Press, 1993).

Stanley Wells, *Shakespeare: The Poet and his Plays* (London: Methuen, 1997).

Stanley Wells and Gary Taylor, *William Shakespeare: A Textual Companion* (Oxford: Clarendon Press, 1987).

Acknowledgements

The author would like to thank Richard Appignanesi, Jeffrey Kahan, Beth Kaye and Marina Warner, and dedicates this book to his family.
The illustrator would like to thank Richard Appignanesi and Oscar and dedicates this book to his parents, sisters and Silvina.

Index